SURVIVING THE KHMER ROUGE GENOCIDE

Growing Up as Everything Began

a true story

KC Ung

Library of Congress Cataloging-in-Publication Date has been applied for
ISBN: 979-8-9894750-0-1

For more information contact: KC Ung
                Email: kc@myselffree.com
                www.myselffree.com
                Edited by: Ryan S. Searcy
                        Kevin Ung
                        Victoria Ung

D e d i c a t i o n

To My Parents

who constantly strived to ensure my safety amidst

the horror of the Khmer Rouge regime.

Your resilience and determination served as a guiding light
during darkness giving me strength to endure the trials that
befell us.

To my dear little sister

Though I can not hold you in my arms, I always carry you
with me. Your spirit lives on in my heart, and you will
forever hold a special place in my thoughts.

Author's Note

After more than a decade of contemplation, I have finally found the courage to write and share my personal story. The decision was greatly influenced by the encouragement received from numerous individuals during my earlier years when I had the opportunity to speak in various programs for international classrooms.

Every time I had the privilege to share my story, I witnessed the profound impact it had on individuals in unique and meaningful ways. Through these interactions, I realized the power of storytelling and its potential to inspire and uplift others facing their hardships.

If my story could offer even a glimmer of hope or support to just one person, then it was a story that needed to be shared. I am not alone in facing difficulties in life, and by sharing my experience, I hope to contribute to a collective of resilience and perseverance.

There are countless individuals out there who may be on the verge of giving up or feeling overwhelmed by life's challenges. It is my sincere hope that by sharing my story, I can serve as a beacon of hope and encouragement for those who may be searching for inspiration or a reminder that they are not alone.

This journey of writing my personal story has been a deeply reflective and cathartic process. It has allowed me to delve into the depths of my experience. Uncovering valuable honesty and vulnerability, aiming to capture the essence of my journey and the emotions that accompanied it.

I am grateful for the support and encouragement I have received from loved ones, and readers who have inspired me to share my story with the world. It is my sincerest hope that my words can make a positive difference in someone's life and ignite a sense of resilience and determination within them.

In conclusion, I believe that our stories have the power to unite, heal, and empower. By sharing our experiences, we create a tapestry of shared humanity that reminds us of our interconnectedness. May my story serve as a reminder that no matter how difficult life may seem, there is always hope and the possibility of a brighter tomorrow.

Thank you for joining me on this journey and may we all find strength and inspiration in the stories that connect us.

Thanks for reading!

Please add a short review on Amazon and let me know what you think!

CONTENTS

1

The Beginning of 1975

Bang, bang, bang, boom…

These were the sounds of bullets and bombs dropped somewhere in the district of Mongkol Borei. These were the sounds that had awoken all of us in the middle of the night. We were overcome with terror, worrying whether these sounds were coming from the other side of town or right across the street. I prayed for this unrelenting barrage to end.

Mongkol Borei is a district in the province of Banteay Meanchey in southwestern Cambodia. It's approximately 358 kilometers, 5 hours drive to Phnom Penh, the capital of

Cambodia. The population of Mongkol Borei occupied a residency of approximately forty-five thousand people in 1975.

In the '70s, I was a young teenager occupying one of those forty-five thousand spots. Like many other kids, all I knew was getting up early in the morning, going to school, and doing chores in and out of the house. I didn't care much about who ran the country if it didn't affect how I lived my day-to-day life.

During this time, Prince Norodom Shihanou was the leader of the country. When I was twelve, I was one of the students chosen by my sixth-grade teacher to welcome the prince when he visited our college in town. I didn't care about who the prince was or his political agenda, but I was excited to be one of the few children selected for this opportunity.

I was too young to understand or even care about politics, but I do remember that it was March 18th, 1970, when Prince Norodom Sihanouk was deposed by Lon Nol and his coup. The prince eventually relinquished his power in 1972.

Lon Nol declared martial law, dissolved the National Assembly, and suspended the Constitution when he took power. He proclaimed that these actions were necessary to keep the country in order and prevent a Communist takeover of the nation

While he was the president of the country, Lon Nol attempted to suppress the Khmer Rouge (Khmer Krohom, in Cambodia). As a result, he plunged the country into a civil war. The war between Lon Nol and the Khmer Rouge had been going on for several years. Communist Khmer Rouge had taken control of one province at a time. Eventually, the Khmer Rouge retained firm control of the Northeast provinces, which included Mongkol Borey, and most of the countryside. More and more territory fell into Communist hands over the next few years

We could often hear battles going on day and night between Lon Nol's troops and the Khmer Rouge. Bombs would explode during the busiest time of the day in Phnom Penh, injuring and killing masses of people at a time. News about the war was constantly updated on television and the radio. At that time, only a select few wealthier families could afford a television. The rest would be listening to radios.

We heard on the radio that the Khmer Rouge were sneaking into towns in the middle of the night. They would kidnap residents, force them into the woods outside of town, and train them to become one of their soldiers. If one refused to abide by their demands, he or she would be executed on the spot.

All the news that had been circulating and happening filled our hearts with sorrow and distress. The pure unfiltered horror was being seen with our very eyes. This couldn't even be compared to a nightmare. We went to sleep with the fear that in a heartbeat, all of us could have died. There was no telling who or where would be targeted next. Everyone was forced to gamble with their own lives. At any moment, our neighboring village could have been bombed and we would be in pure panic. We had to be ready every second of every day, so we slept with a backpack next to us that carried some food and water just in case we had to flee in the middle of the night.

Just like many other towns, the sound of gunshots can be heard every day in Mongkol Borey. The sound of guns got closer and closer as the days went by. The sound of bombs began to echo in our heads. A couple of nights of every week, the gunshots that seemed only a village away or a couple of miles away began inching their way closer and closer. Our bodies became paralyzed with the mere idea of being caught. We would get together with others and sneak away to hide in a rice field about a mile away as a safety precaution, then return home the next morning.

One day, in the beginning of 1975, children began disappearing from school. Parents were petrified of sending their children off for fear that they would never see them again. They could be kidnapped or killed for all they knew. Nobody did any kind of business or work anymore. Every

—

4

night was a sleepless night. Parents would get together daily to discuss any possibility of safety. What was the village supposed to do if the Khmer Rouge invaded our town? What would happen if stray bullets entered our neighborhood? There were endless concerns.

There was so much desperation for safety that every family built a mound in their house to stay safe. That was the best solution everyone had at the time. It was like a bulletproof room, and it was there just for safety. In one of the rooms on the first floor of my home, bags of sand were placed perpendicular to the walls with numerous layers to prevent any gunshots from getting in. There were mass amounts of bottled water and some dried food just in case we needed to hide and survive, for at minimum, a few days.

The fear that the Khmer Rouge would take control of our town and kill the innocent had made people in Mongkol Borei decide to make the next move for their safety. As a result, people who had friends or families in the bigger city had moved to the bigger cities. People without friends or families in the bigger cities tried anything to get there. It was the safest place to be at the time and it gave hope to people. They believed that a bigger city besides Phnom Penh was a safer place for their families because the Khmer Rouge would not dare to sneak in the middle of the night or attack any major cities. Some families moved to the border of Thailand because if things got out of hand, they could make a quick escape to Thailand. My parents were one of those who had planned to move to the border as well.

In just a couple of weeks, Mongkol Borei became a ghost town. More than half of the population in the town had moved to somewhere else. Some families would have one or two members that would stay behind to protect their belongings. Some were left not behind. After a long search for a location for our family, my dad finally found a place for my mom, sisters, and brothers in Ou Chrov, a small town on the border of Thailand. The people who had lived there seemed either uninterested or unconcerned about the activity of the Khmer Rouge and they were leading normal lives.

It was a medium-sized wooden house in the countryside that fit just enough for our family. My father bought it with some of his savings. Even though there were not many people left in town, my father did not want to abandon the home and the business that he had worked hard for. He wanted to stay behind to keep an eye on his property. He wanted to have at least one of his children stay with him. Unfortunately for me, my father and I, along with one of my younger brothers, stayed behind at our home in Mongkol Borei while mom and the rest of my seven siblings lived and left for safety. My dad told us that we had to wait for Mom to settle into the new home first before we could all move in together.

—

We waited for my mom and older brother to settle in and start a small business, so we at least had somewhat of an income. Hopefully, my mother would settle down quickly enough for us to leave. We weren't lucky enough and my mother had not settled down before the railroad from Mongkol Borei to Ou Chrov was destroyed by the Khmer Rouge. We could not believe what happened. No one was allowed to travel between Ou Chrov and Mongkol Borei until the government felt that it was safe to reopen and repair. We were now stuck in Mongkol Borei, and it was up to fate to decide when it was time for us to be reunited.

Every night before I went to sleep, I would pray that the roads would reopen. I could only hope that one day we would be reunited. As the days continued, the roads were still closed because there was still a fear of bombing or an ambush appearing out of nowhere. At first, my closest friend moved to the city with her family. Soon after that, everyone started leaving daily, and people slowly crept out of the town. Mongkol Borey became a ghost town with no one there except us and a few other families without anywhere else to go.

Then one morning, a friend of my parents came to our home. She told my father about the news that she just heard. The Khmer Rouge would invade Mongkol Borei in the next few days and she did not want to take any chances. She would take the remaining members of her family to Battambang on that same day. Battambang is a city Southwest of Phnom Penh, about 293 km, a five-hour drive. My father asked her to take me and my younger brother along to one of his old friends who also lived in Battambang. He felt that my brother and I would be much safer with them than where we were now without even asking for my opinion. She agreed and my father wrote a letter for me to give to his friend when I got there.

I lived with a stranger far away from home and far away from my family. The people I stayed with were very nice. They did the same things my parents did, but it still felt as if they were a completely different race. I felt as if I was alienated from what I was and what I did. They were good friends of my father, but to me, they were some random people who decided to take me in because they pitied me. No matter how friendly they were, I just could not feel comfortable. Even though I did not like where I was, I was always afraid that one day they would just kick me out, and then I would be completely alone without my parents or anyone.

A few days later, my father came to visit me. All my hopes had resurfaced, and I finally felt happy again. My eyes lit up and I had a smile that stretched so far and for so long when he came. I wanted him to stay with me or take me back to our home. I told him that I didn't feel comfortable here. My father told me that I would be safer here and that he needed to go back, and he would take my younger brother back with him, and for me, I must stay. He needed to know as soon as possible when the road from Ou Chrov to Mongkol Borei opened so that we could join my mother and brothers. Then we could all go home and be a family again. I had no choice, so I was forced into agreeing with him due to the dangerous situation around us.

My parent's friends were very generous to me. I was often very worried and just sat thinking. When I did, they would attempt to have me do an activity, but I was just unable to. I kept thinking about what was going on what was going to happen to me and my family and if I was ever going to see them again.

As a few more days passed by, they told me that they heard on the radio that the road between Battambang and Mongkol Borei was bombed. The road was destroyed and was not drivable. No more cars were allowed to travel on the side of the road because the Khmer Rouge was attempting to ambush the people. My lungs suddenly started to fail me, and my mouth was gasping for air. So many thoughts raced through my mind and everything around me slowly started to turn black.

After what seemed like hours, I slowly regained consciousness. My vision returned and I started looking at everything around me; wondering what had recently happened. I suddenly remembered everything, and I started to cry. I wailed and my eyes eventually burned from crying so much. My hosts began getting very upset with me and told me it was useless to cry and that the only thing I could do was sit and pray. They said that if I prayed, everything would work out just right. Every day after that, I prayed and listened to the radio all day long hoping that it would give me an ounce of hope or anything to hold on to.

Time passes by and I still pray and listen to the radio. Falling asleep every night to the radio did no good for me at all. The radio brought nothing except emptiness to my heart and I could not stand it. It has been almost a month and still nothing good at all. All I heard was how more places were getting bombed and more provinces were taken over by the Khmer Rouge and I started to worry more. I felt so useless and alone that I gave up doing everything around the house. I lost my appetite and just sat around all day listening to the radio. My hosts would talk to me every day for either not doing anything or for support. Lying on the couch all day was the only thing I could do. Every day I had such a good feeling that something was going to change, but it never did. By then, I missed my parents and my family. All I could think of was what life was like before all of this happened, and I just wanted to go home.

2

Seeing Khmer Rouge for The First Time – The Worst Just Started

One early morning around 3 am, I awoke to the noise of pots and pans and loud cheering. I heard people screaming with joy and everything sounded so…good. I got up quickly and ran to my window to see what was happening. All I saw was a crowd of people all dressed in black with long guns behind their backs. They had colorful scarves around their neck and some of them wrapped the scarves around their heads. There were miles of them parading on the street. Some were walking on the street; some were riding in army tanks and army trucks. They all kept repeating.

"Jeiyo Brotest Kampuchea, Barajew Lon Nol "in Cambodian, (Victory Cambodia, Defeat Lon Nol). My hosts ran into my room and told me that they were the Khmer Rouge. They had just taken over Phnom Penh, the capital of Cambodia, and controlled the country.

That was the first time that I saw the Khmer Rouge. They looked just like us. I thought, somehow, they had red skin. In Cambodia, the words "Khmer Krohom", translate to "Cambodian" and "red"

Every Cambodian citizen watched the parade on every major street in Battambang and some of the citizens banged pots and pans to cheer along with the Khmer Rouge, the five-year-long war was finally over. I was happy as well because I thought that I could go back home with my family. I did not think that anyone could sleep at this moment, including me.

A few hours later a friend of my parents, the same woman that took me here, visited me. She told me now that the war was over, she and her family would be going back to Mongkol Borei, and she wanted to know if I had any messages to send to my father. I did not want to send any messages, but rather I wanted to go back with them. She kept refusing to say that she did not have enough room and that the car was packed with members of her family and their luggage. I wanted to go so badly that I started to cry. All I could picture in my mind was me going back to my parents and our reunion. I was just so stubborn that everything she said went in one ear and out the other. She kept saying that she would come back next time to get me or that there was no room at all in the car. Everything she said I just tuned out of my mind, and I knew that this "next time" meant never because there was no reason for her to come back. I was not her daughter, and I simply was not worth the drive. I refused to take no for an answer, so I continued to cry begging her to let me go with her and I even told her that I was willing to sit on top of the car roof. Reluctantly, she finally gave up and let me come along.

I was so excited, and I hugged her so tight that I could have crushed her lungs. I ran to my room and packed everything as fast as I could ran back down and jumped on her one more time with another hug. I went to say goodbye to my hosts, but they were hesitant to let me go because they had not heard anything from my father, and I was their responsibility. I was shattered, but I kept my hopes up. I had come this far, and I knew that I would not let anything get in my way of going home. I kept begging and pleading my case and finally, I won them over. I told them that I would take full responsibility for whatever happened to me, and I thanked them gratefully for their hospitality and for letting me stay there. I then ran out the door and I followed the woman to her car.

It took us a while to walk to the car due to the excessive amount of people on the street and sidewalk celebrating. When we got to the car, I did not see anything except a pack of people and luggage. As she said, there was absolutely no room in the car at all and I had to sit on someone's lap. It meant nothing to me because if I could come along, that was enough for me. I was even willing to sit on top of the car roof, I meant it.

The rugged road was nearly impossible to drive and was still closed because of that. There was no way of passing because of all the debris that inhabited the environment which caused a lot of problems. The driver had no choice but to drive off the road. That meant he had to drive on the rice field alongside the road. It was about a two-and-a-half-hour drive to come back home if we were on the regular road, but because of the bombings, the driver feared going through that route, so he took the alternative way, and it was about an 4 hours' drive.

On the way home from Battambang to Mongkol Borei through the rice field, it was so quiet. Throughout the whole rice field, we were the only car that drove by. The field was completely silent and felt as if some Khmer Rouge were about to jump out and exterminate what hopes we had left of going home. We all slowly became struck with fear and could barely move, let alone speak. Everywhere we turned another body was mutilated in some odd way, it was a painful sight to see. The driver did whatever he could to avoid driving over those dead bodies. When avoiding was impossible, we could hear each organ being splattered as we drove over them. The bodies all came to be because they were either shot or died by the bomb/landmines. Everyone prayed and hoped that there were no more landmines left. At that very moment, we all looked into each other's eyes and said goodbye in our minds. The Khmer Rouge was merciless and would do anything they wanted. We were nothing to them, just pawns on a chessboard and it caused us so much fear that we were not going to see all the people that we loved again. The driver drove closer to the highway to make sure that he could see how it went. The highway was much safer than the fields because troops have been known to hide in the field to ambush people. Hopefully, there won't be too many people and we could make it for just a few more hours.

About four hours later, we finally reached the border of Mongkol Borei. All of us were just so relieved that we finally reached the border and that there was nothing more to worry about. I became a little more unperturbed and my once tense body finally relaxed. During the whole trip, I was unable to move because there was no room, and we all were too afraid to move.

As the car was about to enter the town, we saw a group of Khmer Rouge from a distance. They saw our car as we approached town. They gave us a signal to stop the car by firing a shot into the air and our relaxed bodies froze again. The sound of the gun filled us with trepidation. We gazed into each other's eyes fearing the end of our lives. The driver slowed the car down and we finally came to a stop. The Khmer Rouge troops quickly approached and pointed the guns at us. They started screaming at us to get out of the car and I knew that I should have been brave, but I just was not able to muster up the courage needed. They told us to stand in a line and searched every one of us to make sure that we did not carry any weapons. They wanted to make sure that we were not Lon Nol officers or family members. They wanted to know who we were, what we were doing, and where we came from. We told them that we lived here in Mongkol Borei and that we were coming back home.

After they had finished searching and interrogating us, they discussed quietly among each other what they were going to do with us. The woman who picked me up started to tear up a little bit, fearing that it was almost the end. We had no idea what they were going to do to us and why they stopped us in the first place. Were they going to kill us? What was

---

going to happen next? So many questions started to bubble in the back of our minds and about twenty minutes later, they decided to let us go. They told us to take our belongings and to leave right away. They said that they were keeping the car and that the Ungar Leer (referring to their government) needed to borrow the car. We were confused but decided not to question it. We were just happy that they let us go. We gathered our belongings as quickly as possible out of fear of them changing their minds.

What would take us fifteen minutes by car, took us another hour before we finally arrived. I waited for this moment for so long that I could not believe everything I saw. It was a dream come true to see everything the same as it was before. People like us were coming back to town and the once-ghost town of Mongkol Borei was finally vivacious again. We went to their home first because my house was on the other side of the Mongkol Borey River, so it would take me another half hour to walk to the bridge to get home. I was completely exhausted by then, but I kept on walking because I knew that this was what I wanted.

The bridge was not that long, but from their house to the bridge and from the bridge to my home, it was a good walking distance. I did not want to hinder my journey home, so I looked down the river and the water was just shallow enough for me to walk through it. When I was younger, I would play in the river all the time, so it was normal for me to walk through the river. Cutting through the river saved me from passing out because it cut out at least another half an hour's walk. The river was about as high as my waist, so it was not that bad at all. I put my bag on top of my head. It took me about fifteen minutes to cross the river. I ran through the river as fast as I could, not caring how much I splashed or how wet I got.

When I arrived home around six pm, I was drenched with water. It was less than five hundred feet to get home; I stood there for a few minutes just embracing the moment. I finally was able to see people that I had not seen for so long. It seems my parents sat in front of the house with many other neighbors and some small children playing around them. I also saw my oldest sister, her husband, and their one-year-old son there as well. My sister lived with her husband in "Serei Saophoan" which was less than a thirty-minute drive from Mongkol Borey.

I walked in slowly. I yelled out that I was home and suddenly, I heard, and I finally felt safe again. My mom embraced me and did not let go. I could tell by the look in her eyes that she was relieved too. My mother told me that she arrived a few hours ago. I heard footsteps scurrying to the front door. They were my brothers and sisters. They all looked at me with such relief as well. Then my parents started

---

questioning me about how I was drenched in water, and she wanted to know how I got home. I told her about my journey through the rice fields and what happened at the border, and I could tell how worried she got. I got so wrapped up in my own story that I kept going on and on. She just told me that whatever happened passed and that we should look ahead now. There were no more fears of bombing and no more fears of anything now.

I went upstairs to my room, and everything was still the same. Besides a few layers of dust collecting on all my things, my room looked like an old picture that I had kept in my pocket all this time. We all sat in front of the house talking about what we went through and how the war affected each one of us. Our lives were so different, yet it was all the same. We all went through so many different things but held on to the same values and that is what kept us all alive and together. It seemed like there was so much to talk about that made everyone stay up late that evening. My sister and her husband went home to Serei Saophoan, but they left her one-year-old child to spend time with us.

The next morning, it was still very early; about five am. Everyone was asleep at the same time, and I was too. It was the first night in a very long time that I was able to sleep on my bed again. We were all awakened by a loud announcement on the microphone. The Khmer Rouge was driving all over town to make the announcement. They told us that there were many bombs hidden around town and it was very dangerous for everyone. They need to evacuate all of us out of town as soon as possible. They wanted us to get out of our home, from our town, no later than noon and that they would not be responsible for any people that still were around town after noon. They told us that we only needed to pack for three days. After three days, we would be able to come back. The word "bomb" scared all of us. We thought that it was all safe, but not even a whole day had gone by, and we were already in danger again. We did not want to take any chances, so we packed only the necessary items that were needed for everyday living. Since they told us that we only needed to stay out of town for three days, most of us would pack for those three days. We were ordered to get out of town at a minimum of ten kilometers away and that they would let us know when it was ready for us to go back.

3

The Evacuation

Even before the sun rose, people started to get out of town as soon as they could. Some families used their cars as transportation to carry their belongings while other people used their bicycles and motorcycles. Others had to walk and carry their belongings on their shoulders. Since my father was in the transportation business, we used one of our trucks to carry our food and supplies. Since we had so much space in the truck, we packed more than three days worth of items. My parents had also offered a ride to the neighbors. By about 10 am, the streets of Mongkol Borei were flooded with people rushing out to leave town. There were miles and miles of people marching away from their hometown once again.

After what seemed like endless hours of driving due to the excessive amount of people everywhere, we finally arrived at our destination. We arrived at the countryside called "Phnom Buntew Neag", which was approximately ten kilometers south of Mongkol Borei. The Khmer Rouge were waiting for us already and they told us to stop and look for a place to stay. This countryside was very small and did not have many houses so many people were unfortunate. Whoever was able to find a small house attempted to temporarily move in with the owners, while people who were not as lucky took shelter under trees or under the bare sun.

Because of our predicament, we thought that we would be able to use our truck as a shelter, but we were wrong. Immediately after we arrived at Phnom Buntew Neag, the Khmer Rouge ordered anyone with cars or trucks to leave them behind because now the Khmer Rouge owned them. They all belonged to them now and we had no say in it. We were irritated and angry, but we were too scared to disobey so we just gave them what they wanted. We unloaded our belongings as quickly as possible, but we did not have enough time to unload all the extra food that we had carried as provisions. Since we did not have a truck anymore, we were forced to search for a place to stay. We had been searching until my legs felt as if they were about to fall apart when we finally found a family that allowed us to stay on their front porch.

My parents, along with many other families, realized that everything they worked hard for would soon be gone. What we thought was a blessing was slowly becoming poison in disguise. Everyone still had hope though. Even though we doubted it, we still had faith that the Khmer Rouge would let us go back home to our old lives. It was only a few days anyway, what could they have done to us?

Since we were not allowed to have a car or truck anymore, the only transportation that we could own was bicycles. Suddenly the bicycle is the most valuable transportation to all of us. That made my older brother (two years older than me) wanted to go back home to get his bicycle. My parents did not permit him to go; it was too dangerous. He insisted that he must go. It would be the only transportation for us to have. It didn't matter much how dangerous it might be, he must go. If we didn't have one, then walking would be our only means of getting around. Not to mention that a bike would help us carry many things. Since one of his friends had a bike and offered him a ride, it would not take too much time for them to get there. He decided to go with him because he needed to retrieve something from his home. My parents were too worried and kept saying "No" and that it was not important enough to risk his life. He kept on insisting and promised to be careful. He told them that he would rush home as soon as possible to prevent any possible casualty. My parents finally agreed, and off he went.

After my brother left, my parents started pacing back and forth until it began to make me worried. That was all they did while they waited for my brother. After several hours, my brother finally returned with his bicycle and some of our gardening tools. He told us that there was nothing left in our town. There were no people, and it was completely empty, except for a few guards. With his stealth, he said he was able to avoid being seen and swiftly got his bike from our house. He thought someone was coming so he left through the backdoor when he saw a few more guards appear out of nowhere. He ran to a bush in the backyard of our house and hid for a few minutes until they were gone, and he told us that he heard that we might be forced to farm. We all were shocked, and we started to get even more worried than we already were. What happened to us just staying here for three days?

And what would happen to me if I remained with his friend in Battambang? I would properly never see my family again. If the Khmer Rouge evacuated us here in Mongol Bori, I was certain that it occurred in Battambang and numerous other areas. It disturbed me just to think about it.

———

My one-year-old nephew remained with us all this time. His parents probably were stressed by such a huge concern over how he was and where we were currently. I assumed that she, her significant other, and their inlaw had been evacuated also, however, where were they expelled to?

We only had one day of safety and after that first day, our lives completely changed. We were forced to revert to surviving the way our ancestors did years ago and we were practically present-day peasants. Our bathroom facilities would be in the woods that were close by and the only way to have light or a fire to cook would be by making our fire with logs. We were forced to walk for miles just to find some water because there were no nearby streams that we could drink out of. We also did not have any beds, so we made do with the floor. The first few nights, many people had trouble adapting because there were so many mosquitoes and just so many bugs overall. Thankfully for us and a few other families, we had a mosquito net, so we were protected. These were just a few things that we were forced to adopt immediately.

Three days felt like a millennium to everyone. Every day seems like it would prolong itself just because of the temptation of going home. Finally, the third day arrived, and everyone was excited that we were finally returning to Mongkol Borey. Instead, though, the Khmer Rouge told us that they needed more time to clean up and that they would let us know as soon as it would be ready. No one could believe what just happened, but we had nothing to say back so we just dealt with it. Another few days and it would be done, we all said to ourselves. We just believed that we would eventually go home. Fortunately for us, it had not rained yet, so we were lucky. Days continued to pass and still, there was no word of when we could go back. People began to run out of food and had trouble, but the majority still had some money, so they bought food from people who already lived in the countryside.

One morning, the Khmer Rouge announced that every family would need to attend a meeting. We all thought that it was finally time to go home, so many people packed all their belongings and got ready for good news. When we all gathered for the meeting, they told us that we would need to move another ten kilometers further, including the residents that were already living in the countryside because where we were staying was not a safe place. They said there was still a possibility of getting hurt from the bombs back at home. This time they told us exactly where to go, and when we arrived there, we had to register to let them know our name. We were forced to give them all our personal information, such as our profession, how many people in our family, how many males or how many females, and how old everyone was so they could provide us with a proper amount of food.

Our fear of not being able to go became a reality; our hearts and souls were just taken away by the Khmer Rouge. We knew that this was just the beginning. But we had to be strong to keep on going and not give up hope. It was easier said than done. Many elderly start to faint from the news.

Since our bags were already packed from the previous evacuation, we just continued walking in the same direction as ordered by the Khmer Rouge. It was miles and miles and many people kept walking out of Buntew Neang. It was exactly like before, except now there were no cars. My parents were extremely grateful to my brother because he had the guts to go back home to obtain his bicycle. Thanks to him, we did not need to carry as much because we could just throw a few heavy things on the bicycle. The journey took almost a full day of walking and when we finally arrived at the location, it was the Mongkol Borei Riverbank. We all spread out and tried to find a spot to stay as fast as we could. Our family ended up staying with another family under a palm tree. The tree could provide us with some shade during the day. We had to adapt our lives to the way the communists wanted us to live. From sleeping on the bed inside our home to sleeping on the ground under a palm tree.

4

Living by the Riverbank Under the Palm Tree

A s soon as we put our bags down, we were approached by a few Khmer Rouge. They started interrogating us and asked for general information such as our name, age, and gender again. They also asked a lot about our family background and what we had done in the past. Along with that, they told us to be at their meeting in about an hour and to make sure that every member of the family was in attendance. At this point, when we heard the word "MEETING", we did not like it at all. When we arrived at the meeting, everyone was categorized by their sex and age into four different groups. The elderly women were called "Mea" which meant mother, and all the elderly men were called "Pouk", which meant father. The young girls were called "Bhon Srey" which meant younger sister "Bong Strey" which meant big sister and the boys were called "Bhon Bros", which means younger brother, and "Bong Bros" which meant big brother.

They told us that we were all family and from then on, we were united and equal. To us though, we did not know what this meant so we just followed along because it sounded friendly and respectful. We were all generally separated into two groups: us and The Khmer Rouge. Everyone referred to the Khmer Rouge as the "Ungar Leer", which meant that they were the authorities. If we were the same age as them, they would call us "meth" which means a male friend, or "meth neary" for a female.

Because they did not want individualism, women young and old were forced to cut their hair to the length of the bottom ears. There was to be nothing different, and we were all to look generally the same. As for the males, they needed to have a buzz cut. If we did not obey, they said that they would sever our throats with palm tree leaves. The palm leaf was like a rose's thorn. On the side, it zigzagged, and it was extremely rouge. People used it as a knife sometimes to cut mangoes when a knife was not nearby.

Everyone began to become frightened every day. No one could ever tell who they could trust and who they should fear. From what we witnessed, no one was equal at all. It felt like we were in a feudalist era, and we were the peasants. As time went by, rumors started to emerge. At first, the officers only told us to be quiet. As time continued to pass by, more and more people started to daze off or talk about other things. One of the soldiers got very upset and shot into the air. Everyone jumped and was immediately silent. We all were too overcome with fear to move. Even the babies in the crowd stopped crying and were paralyzed with fear.

We were petrified and all we could do was wonder what was going to happen next. It felt as if time stopped, and it was just like a movie. The suspense kept building up and we did not know what was going to hit us next. After a few minutes of silence, they continued by telling us that we were not allowed to wear colorful clothing. Scarves were the only thing that was allowed to be colorful and therefore anything colorful that we owned would need to be plain. What many people ended up doing was picking a few leaves and smashing them. They then rubbed it all over the clothes to make a bland greenish type of stain. Our once bright and happy clothes were now dark and depressing.

They informed us that males and females were restricted from wearing any shorts because the authorities thought that it was used for seduction, therefore it was a criminal offense to wear those types of clothing. Since we did not bring many clothes with us, we had to use whatever we had to extend our shorts. Many people had trouble with this and because they were so afraid, they were willing to pay other people to make them longer. If we had short-sleeved shirts or short pants, we would find a fabric to extend the sleeves, but where could we find any kind of fabric? We were by the riverbank under the palm trees and there was absolutely nothing around us. We had no choice but to cut other pieces to extend the ones that we would wear.

They also told us that from now on, we did not have any homes for ourselves anymore. They said that where we lived now was our home and that this was it. Whatever we made and whatever we built was all we had left. They told us that if they decided for us to go somewhere else, they would tell us at least a day in advance. Everyone was heartbroken because parents who worked hard for their whole life suddenly lost everything in an instant. Just by those words they said, people's worlds collapsed, and their sense of security faded. Now no one knew what was going to happen next and what we all were going to do next. We had to live one day at a time.

By this time, everything we had was lost. They took all our personal belongings, and we were unaided and unable to stop them. They only told us what to do and where to live from then on. Because of our predicament, all the adults gathered to figure out what they could do, but it was hopeless. Nobody wanted to take any risks because we did not know what they were capable of yet and what they could do to us. Many of the people had families and were too afraid to stand up to any of the Khmer Rouge troops because of the thought of what might happen to them. They may not ever recover, and their family might acquire problems with the troops because of them. All we could do was live it out and hope that everyone would make it, even though everyone knew deep in their hearts that it would not happen.

In the meantime, my father had talked to us about the possibility of owning farm animals. Because of the current events, he thought that we might need to adapt to survive. If we worked as farmers, we would need any help that we could obtain to get the work done. Every member of our family looked at him with our chins dropped down to the floor. We were speechless, and it felt so awkward that my father would even consider being a farmer, especially after the lives that we had. We were one of the luckier families who were able to buy things we wanted from time to time and suddenly, we were about to do manual labor.

The word "farmer" was just a big surprise to us, and we knew that for however long the Khmer Rouge would have trouble getting by. My father knew immediately what we were thinking and told us that we needed to think diversely. He said that we needed to accumulate different abilities because of what was going on. All I could think of was how a businessman was suddenly forced to be a farmer to support his family.

While we were waiting for the authorities to decide where we would stay, they gave us uncooked rice and salt for our food. They gave each family a certain amount of food depending on the amount of people in each family. Each person would receive one twelve-ounce can of uncooked rice per day and a cup of salt per family. There was no meat or vegetables because they were considered a "luxury" and we were not able to have that. They told us that we only needed the essentials for living. If we wanted any meat or vegetables, we would have to hunt or look for it ourselves.

This was all we had, and the fact that we were a large family did not help our problems. We needed to get hold of mass amounts of food to feed ourselves. Since we stayed by the riverbank, we, along with other families, immediately thought of fish. My brothers and I would go fishing and hope that we would catch something. We used to go out with our mosquito net and catch fish that way. What we did was hold both ends of the net and go as far away from each other as we could without stretching the net. Because the river was low, we were able to stand in it. We pulled the net away from each other and just stood there hoping that the fish would come. From time to time, we would walk upstream a little hoping that some unfortunate fish would get caught in our net and that we would finally catch something.

5

Catching Fish with A Mosquito Net

After a few hours of waiting, we did not get anywhere. We did not catch any fish because many other families were doing what we were doing, and they were standing further upstream. My brother and I were tired. We felt so discontented, and we just wanted to give up. Along with that, we also got hungry, so we went to get the lunch that our mother had packed for us. We sat down looking at the river because we felt so discouraged. This was our first time fishing, and there was absolutely nothing that came remotely close to our net. Besides, our family depended on us to catch fish for food. Even though I used to play in the river when I was a child, I never had to catch fish, so this was a difficult task. It felt endless and we just did not know what else to do. While eating our lunch, we contemplated how we could try again. We started to observe how other families fished and tried to see if we could mimic them.

Following our lunch, my brother suggested that we go down the river further in hopes that we would finally catch something. He thought that because there were fewer people, there would be a higher chance of catching fish. Along with that, there were more bushes and things for all the fish to hide in. It seemed logical that more fish would be hiding and that they would be there because there was no other place that they could be. Both of us hoped so strongly that we could show our parents that we were able to help provide. This inspired us to do the best that we could do.

After only a while of searching, we found a nice-looking spot. It was quiet with no people around and there were few little bushels inside the river. We were a little scared by ourselves far away from the others, but our enthusiasm for finding this location was greater than fear. We did not want to waste any time and we just ran there. We quickly got our net ready and slowly approached the bushes. As we got closer and closer, we began to hear a splashing sound under the bushes, and my brother and I were just so happy. Our smiles stretched across our faces, and we knew we were lucky. We surrounded the bush and threw a few pebbles into it to lure the fish out and into our net. They began to swim around the net and because walking in a river is different from walking on land, we missed many fish and ended up only catching a few big ones. Even with our few catches, we were happy. We took it out of the river and sat on the bank looking at what we caught. It was so amazing because there was such a variety. We thought that we only caught fish, but there were so many more things such as crabs and shrimp in there. We threw them in the bucket and began our hunt for fish again. It was almost sunset; my brother and I did not want to leave. Because of our recent achievements, we felt like pros at fishing. It was just so enjoyable, and we had so much fun. Neither of us wanted to leave, but we left because we knew that it was late and that our parents would begin to worry soon.

My parents were so surprised to see the bucket full of fish. They attempted to hide their feelings from us, but I could see through their eyes that they had never thought in a million years that their teenage children would be supporting them. My mind was telling me how I should change the subject before they started to cry tears of happiness. We ended up telling them how we were able to catch a variety of sea creatures. My mother started to clean up the fish. Since we had so many, my mother salted the extra fish and hung them under the sun to dry for later use. Within an hour, word spread like wildfire about how much we caught and the diversity of our findings. The next morning, other people began to follow us to infiltrate our tricks for catching fish. It did not take long for people to take over our spot and catch on to what we were doing.

The wait continued and we still had no idea where we were going to live. In the meantime, the river had fewer fish to catch due to the number of people who fished there every day. Because it was in such a short period, the fish were not able to reproduce fast enough, and they were close to extinction in that river. We wondered what would happen to us because now that we had no more fish, we would be low on food.

Fishes were not the only thing that lived in the river, there were other creatures such as muscles, snails, crabs, and more. But these things were at the bottom of the river. That required us to rely on our feet to search for them. When we felt something unfamiliar, we would reach the bottom with our hands and grab hold of it. With practice, we became adept at methods of successfully finding and collecting various things.

Summer had just begun, and the weather was cooperating with us. Thankfully, there were not any rainy days yet. At night, I would lie down under the palm trees and always fell asleep wondering what would happen if one day it rained.

Where would we sleep? Everything would be muddy and dirty, and we would be forced into many unbearable situations. Millions of questions kept popping into my head every night, but I just was not able to answer any of them.

Later that evening, the Khmer Rouge made their decision for us. They finally decided where we should all live by splitting us all up into a group that consisted of ten families. We were all assigned a group to live within a different part of the countryside with various tasks. I did not know where the other families went, but my family along with the other nine families went far into the countryside along the Mongkol Borei riverbank where there was a village called Phum Sroa Moch with some residents.

Our journey began with us walking on foot and that's all we did, walked on foot. It took us about two days, and it felt like we took a million steps. After that agonizing journey, we finally arrived at Phum Sroa Moch. These were all single homes that were on the riverbank and consisted of approximately five thousand residents. The residents who already lived there had not been affected by the Khmer Rouge yet. Unfortunately, they were about to be. They lived their lives in peace until we came. They had no idea what it was like for us to be evacuated from our own homes. They were just happy to see us because they saw the potential of making money by selling us food.

The village had been divided into two parts of residents, the South and North. The residents on the south side of the village were wealthier than the residents on the north side and all the houses in that village were built at a minimum of fifteen feet above the ground. Underneath the house, there would be plenty of room to walk around. The people in the village told us that all the houses were built high above the ground because they were along the riverbank and when it was high tide season or the rainy season, the houses would be flooded, and people could only travel by boat. People would have handmade canoes that they had just for the rainy season so that everyone could still get around. In addition to that, the flood would continue at least for a minimum of two and half months before it would go away so it was a necessity.

We had no shelter when we arrived, and we were forced to pay for a place to stay. Everyone did not have much money except for some spare change. My family and one of the other families gathered up all of what we had rented a place underneath one of the houses. The people who lived there did not waste any time trying to make money from us. They quickly learned that we had left our home for about two months and did not have good food and we would do anything to eat. One of the women made coconut waffles to sell to the children. Coconut waffles were made with coconut, rice flour, sugar, and yeast. We would stay in line and wait for our turn to buy one from her because this was the first thing that we ate that was just so good in two months.

Most of the residents in Poum Sroa Moch owned at least a pair of cows and a wagon; they used them as transportation for travel to different towns or to take merchandise to sell in the market. The people in the village told us that without the cow and the wagon, life would be very difficult to manage. After a few days of staying in that village, we learned that it was true how life was difficult without a cow or wagon. When we traveled on land, we needed to go through the field, and it was too bumpy to hold many pots and pans. It was next to impossible when trying to ride a bike because the whole trail was not smooth so my family and the one who lived with us tried to obtain them.

My sister and her husband showed up unexpectedly with their motorcycle. She was overwhelmed to find us. She worried and missed her child deeply. She told us that she and her in-laws and other families were evacuated from Serei Saophoan. However, she had been able to keep most of her possessions. They used the motorcycle to travel and look for us while they still had it. Without it was impossible for them to find us. From what she went through it was not as bad as us. Different parts of the country had their authority. We spent several hours catching up before they needed to return to their home and take her child with her. My parents felt relieved as well that their grandkid was united with his parents.

My parents and other families went off to buy the cows and the wagon, but there was a problem. The seller would not accept cash because what they wanted was gold. They told us that they heard a rumor that the communist Khmer Rouge was eradicating the use of money and that it was useless now. It was worth noting that what we had was just paper now, nothing more. We were all confused because we were not sure what they were trying to do. We all thought they were trying to scare us because how would they even know this information? It didn't matter though if the news was true or not. We believed that owning cows and wagons were a must for us. We would do whatever we could to make that happen. My mom decided to take some of her jewelry and had my father exchange them for the cows and wagon. My brother wanted to go along so that he could help my father pick the cows that he liked.

We were waiting impatiently for my father and brother to return. The wait was finally over when I saw my father and brother returning. We were so thrilled with what they brought back, it was the first pair of cows and the first wagon that we had ever owned. It made us feel good that we finally owned something once again with the present situation that was given to us. To my brothers and me, the cows became like our pets. We cleaned them and treated them like members of the family. We made sure that they were always healthy because they provided and meant so much to us.

A few days later, the Khmer Rouge had come and collected bicycles from every family including the residents in the village. They told us that the bicycles belonged to the Ungar Leer and that we were not allowed to own them anymore. Again, we were so mad but could not do anything because we were scared for our lives. They were taking one thing at a time away from us. First, it was our home, then it was our truck, and now it was our bicycles, what else could they take from us next? Were they going to take our cows that we just got? These questions just kept reappearing in the back of our minds as we lingered waiting for what was going to happen next. We were so exasperated but too scared to confront them. Adults gathered and discussed how our lives had been turned upside down by these so-called "rescuers from the war". What could we do?

We lived underneath people's homes for two weeks and the money we had was useless. The rumors from people in the village were correct. The Khmer Rouge had finally announced that the money that once had value would not be recognized anymore. We would become farmers and work for our government (Ugka Leer). There were no rich and poor anymore. We were all equal. There was no need to do any kind of business.

The next morning, the Khmer Rouge had ordered us to move again. This time they wanted us to live in the mountain called "Phnom Goon Domray" (Phnom is the mountain, Goon is a child, and Domray is an elephant). From a distance, the shape of the mountain looked like a baby elephant. It was another day of journey through the fields, and we were lucky to have the cows and wagon to help us carry our belongings. If we did not have them, it would have been very difficult for us to walk in the field and carry all the stuff. It would have taken much longer because we just had so many things that we all needed. So far, we were very happy with the cow and the wagon despite the situation that we were in.

6

Turning the Jungle into Home – The Mountain of Phnom Goon Dumrey

It took us about half a day to arrive. We were heartbroken as soon as we were at the base of the mountain. All we could see was the mountain full of trees and there were no homes and no one ever lived there before. It was a jungle. Right away I was frightened. None of us knew how we were going to live in a place like this. We didn't know if any wild animals could poison or eat us. I was especially horrified because I didn't think that we would make it through this, there was no possible way that we could. My parents and the other adults were about to collapse when they saw the place that was hypothetically our home, but they were all strong because we needed to cope with the situation.

The Khmer Rouge troops led us to the mountain and told us what to do. They gave us some gardening tools and different kinds of seeds to plant and told us to cut the trees down in certain locations and grow corn fields and other crops. They also gave us a good amount of uncooked rice in advance, which meant they would not come to check on us any time soon. We were on our own.

On the mountain, there was no lake or pond nearby for us to use as water. Immediately, we had to work together to make our lives as comfortable as we could. Each family would assign a few of the members of their family to cut trees down right away so that we could build our shelter. We would use tree trunks as the main pole and the tree branches and leaves would be used as the walls and the roof.

Some of us would search for water, but it was hopeless because there was not any around. We had no choice but to dig a hole in the ground and hope that there would be a hidden spring somewhere. Dig after dig and there was still no water at all. We kept trying and switched to different locations in the hope that at least one of them would work. In some of the spots, we would dig as deep as four feet, and still no water. After many tries, we finally dug into the right spot. It was after just about two feet of digging; it was an overwhelming experience to see the water emerge slowly from the ground. We continued to dig deeper so that the water would come out faster. We continued to dig a few more so that we would have plenty of water to use. Toward the end of the day, we had plenty of water to cook and to clean

The first night on the mountain was exhausting. We tried to do as much as we could with shelter before the night arrived, but it was impossible. Everything involved human labor and we could only do so much for each day. So, for the first night, we would sleep on the ground under the tree and it scared so many of us because we still did not know if there were any wild animals around us. Due to our exhaustion, we slept through the whole night.

A few days later, our new temporary homes were finally finished. It looked pretty good based on the material that we had to work with. The only thing that we were concerned with was the rain. We knew for sure that the roof that was built with leaves would not be able to stand the rain, but there was nothing that we could do about that.

From this day on, the mountain "Phnom Goon Domray" would be our town, if we could even call it a town. All we had were houses that we made from tree branches and leaves and that would be our home. To get the essentials, we needed to work hard to get all the basic foods and it was just too difficult. Every day we would wake up as early as five in the morning to get ready for work and we would all split up into different groups to find food.

Any parents or grandparents would stay back at what we called our home. They would prepare food for us to take to work. As soon as we got back from work, we would be forced to work in the garden around our houses too. My brother, along with his friends and other people his age, would search around the mountain to see if they were able to find anything that we could eat as food or if there were any animals that they could hunt for meat. Unfortunately, they endlessly looked, and nothing was found. Instead, they found out that there were wild potatoes that grew on the mountain. My brothers and others went to dig potatoes. Simultaneously, they explored different avenues regarding some wild plants that we could eat as well. About a week later, they found a pond about two hours away that had fish. We were so excited about this because even simple things such as fish became such a luxury to us. We were so accustomed to eating scraps and having that hungry feeling in our stomachs all the time that having a full meal became something everyone could only dream of.

Our jobs were to cut down the trees and pull the weeds that grew on the side of the mountain. We needed to make room for the cornfields and begin to plant corn as soon as possible for the communists. Along with that, corn was our only stable supply of food, so we needed to grow it as soon as possible. Until then, we needed to find a temporary substitute for it.

One afternoon at the work field, it suddenly started to storm. The wind and rain just came out of nowhere and started to blow. The wind was so strong, and it felt like a tornado was about to hit us. Everyone had to stop work early because of the weather. We were walking and it felt like we were running because the wind was just so strong, we felt like it was pushing us. On our way home, many people fell repeatedly due to strong winds. We were helping the people who fell because they just did not have the strength to keep continuing. Out of nowhere, I heard a croak and saw a frog while trying to hold people up. When I looked at it, all I could picture was a warm meal, and I began to drool. I yelled and everyone started to chase the frog. It was every man for themselves and whoever caught the frog would have it. It was next to impossible to catch it when there was this much rain and half of us could barely stand up due to the rain, so it felt hopeless. The thought of even being able to have something real to eat overpowered my thoughts of failure. But the frog jumped too fast, and we kept missing it. After a few minutes, we decided to let it go because the storm was getting stronger, and we needed to get home.

Due to the weather on that day, it took us twice as long to return home. We saw our parents trying to stay dry inside our home. Because of the building materials we had, the roof was leaking very badly and there was just so much water everywhere. In the past, we were always concerned about if it would rain, but now our fears had become a reality. All parents could do was put pots and pans in the spots with the most water. After it was filled, they would just pour it out outside and they kept this up for hours. Thankfully though, we were able to have dinner because my parents had decided to cook dinner early. After all, the weather looked so cloudy.

It continued to rain for the whole night, and we all fell asleep huddled together to stay warm. It was just so cold, and we had no floors except for the cold wet dirt that slowly became mud, and it was just so unbearable. The next morning, we all took our wet clothes to hang under the sun. The weather was back to the way it was, and it was just so hot that we wished that the rain would come back. The weather was always extreme so whatever weather we had; we would eventually want it back. We also fixed up our house by adding more leaves on the existing leaves in hopes that if it rained again, it would not be as bad, and less water would get in. As a precaution, we cut down tree trunks and made thin layers of wood just in case the roof somehow ended up failing on us.

We would have beds that would hopefully not be as cold as the ground.

Every other week, a few of the Khmer Rouge would check up on us to make sure that we did whatever they wanted us to do. Every time they came, they would have a meeting just to tell us how hard they had to fight for us to free us from the war. It was all propaganda, and we knew how fake it was, but no one was brave enough to reject the ideas, so we just went along with it. Everyone was just so miserable that no one could picture a life out of this. They reminded us that we were all equal from now on and that no one was wealthier than another. I just laughed silently in my head because they lived like kings while we were just peasants. They claimed that they slept on the ground and ate the same food that we did, but we all saw them with their hammocks or eating what we could only dream of.

Time passed, and we finally adapted to life in the mountains of "Phom Goon Domray". We were inspired and became more miserable every day of our lives because all we could do was wait and hope that the corn seeds that we planted would grow and feed us. We had other vegetables too such as tomatoes, basil broccoli seeds, but we always had the fear of our plants suddenly dying from the weather, and just like that, we would have to restart. But on the brighter side, we would soon have a variety of food to eat if nothing went wrong.

A couple of months later, everything we had upgraded. Our house looks a lot better, we were reinforced with more leaves and barely had leaks now. The crops were ready to pick, and we all got so much energy from the smell of the crops. We adapted our lives to daily work. We were all so happy and could not wait to harvest our crops. But our enjoyment did not last long when the Khmer Rouge arrived one day and told us that we would have to relocate ourselves and that they were here to take over the mountain. Everyone just sat with sullen looks on their faces because we worked so hard for all of this, and we would not even be able to enjoy any of it. They practically told us to get lost after stealing what we had created. None of us would say anything so we just all took it in. There was nothing that we could do, and we just took the order and relocated.

We were dazed when the Khmer Rouge led us to one of the towns called Preah Netr Preah. The town was like our hometown in Mongkol Borey. We expected that they would escort us to another jungle like Phnom Goun Domrey, but they didn't. When we arrived, none of the residents lived there. It seemed that they had been evacuated from their home just like we had been. They told us to stay in a certain area and just left us there for a few hours. During that time, we saw many more people arrive. We had no idea where they were from originally, but we knew for certain that they had been evacuated from their home as well. The Khmer Rouge finally came back and told us that this was a temporary place for us to stay until they knew for certain where they wanted us to live.

We were allowed to stay in one of those houses and to our knowledge, all the houses in the town were searched by someone for something. The furniture was upside down and everything was just a big mess. By looking at all the messes in the house, we could imagine that our home in Mongkol Borey would look like that too. We were able to find some clothes that we could use that were left behind by their previous owners.

The Khmer Rouge ordered us to register members of our family again for them to provide us with food. They then instructed us to pull weeds from the watermelon field as our new jobs. Every day for about two weeks, we worked in a watermelon field from about 7 am to about 5 pm. When we pulled the weeds out, we found out that there were a few kinds of weeds that were edible. We would pull it out and set it aside so that we could take it home with us after work, so we had something to eat because the Khmer Rouge gave us so little for so many people. We would cook the weeds in the boiling water for a few minutes and then take it out and sprinkle some salt over it for taste.

One evening, the Khmer Rouge declared that they had decided where our permanent home was going to be. We were nervous and wanted to know where we would end up living. Was it going to be in the town, in the mountain, or the jungle? We could not wait to hear what they had to tell us, so we all rushed to the meeting. They told us that from this day on, we would all have a permanent home and there was no need to keep moving anymore. We would live in the real world, and we would help the Ungaleer to make the country more modern, and more powerful, and there would be more food to eat than ever before. As soon as he finished, two troops were assigned to each family, and they were escorted to the destination of their choice. We were terrified to learn that they would decide who we lived with. For these past few months, my family and one of the families that shared the space with us at Phum Sroa Moch had become close friends. To learn that they would separate us was just so frightening. All this time, we supported each other physically and emotionally. Fortunately for them, their family was luckier than us because they were assigned to go back to live in Phum Sroa Moch. At least they knew that it was not a jungle and that the place was decent. For my family, they assigned us to live in the mountain called "Phnom Sress". Our hearts were jumping so fast, and we all were sweating and nervous. When we heard the word Phnom (mountain), right away we were reminded of how the previous mountain looked the first day. It took months just to make it decent looking and it was going to be that all over again.

7

Our New Home – The Village of Phnom Sress

The journey to Phnom Sress was on the field and it was very bumpy. Again, we were lucky to have the cows and the wagon. It only took us half a day with their help, otherwise, it would have taken us much longer and we would have been more tired. It was astonishing to see the mountain from the distance because it was not what we had imagined at all. We could see that there were many coconut and palm trees around the mountain. When we arrived, there was a village on the mountain where people lived. All the houses were built around the base of the mountain and high above the ground. Toward the top of the mountain, there were all kinds of fruit trees such as oranges, lemons, papayas, jackfruit, mangos, and many others.

The people that lived there were expecting us. They were very nice, friendly, and happy to see us. We were the only family that was new to their village. Right away they made us feel comfortable and gave us a place to stay. They allowed us to live in one of their houses, about ten feet by fifteen feet in size. There was just enough room to fit everyone. The whole house was about six feet above the ground six steps later. The floor of the house was built from dark-colored wood, and it was beautiful. The wall was also built from wood and the roof was built with a special kind of haystack that was specially used to protect from the rain. The houses in the whole village had the same kind of roof. There was a big pond about five hundred feet away from our new home. We would have some space close to our home to plant our vegetables. The village was already affected by the Khmer Rouge; however, it was different from us. They were allowed to live in their village and their own home. They were monks and the temple still existed. Up to now, the Khmer Rouge had taken fruit trees and the rice farm from them.

The people in the village told us that the mountain was divided into two parts of the region, the west and the east. They both had their authority. My family lived on the east side and all of us, including the people in the village, were not permitted to cross the border to the west side. We were told by the troops that they would not be responsible for the lives of those who did not obey their order. We wondered why the town was segregated and why they were split into two different groups on one mountain. It made no sense because it should be a unified government under a single mountain. We had questions, but no answers.

The Khmer Rouge highly anticipated that there was a less fortunate economic class before and that there would still be a poorer section of people. Because of their position in society, they wanted to show how they were attempting to equalize people's rights by bringing the most unlikely candidate to a person with power. The reason that the Khmer Rouge wanted to give power to the peasant class was that they believed that these people had less education. They were easily manipulated into doing what the communist party wanted and did not know any better. All they knew was that they needed to survive, and by helping the Khmer Rouge, they would have a better life than they did before. They went from peasants to high-ranking officials who ate glamorous meals every day and had a decent spot to sleep every night. They also went from being one of the villagers to becoming a spy for the communist party. At night they snuck around eavesdropping and tried to find out if any rebellion or any trash talk was going on about the communists. If someone was caught bad-mouthing the communists, they would be beaten in front of the whole village. If someone caught people threatening the idea of communism, they would be taken away and no one would see them again. We all knew what happened to them though. Occasionally, we could hear screams of pain and anguish. The same evening that we arrived, the troops invited us to their meeting, and they told us that the meeting was held once a week and our work would start the next morning.

The following morning, the villagers gathered and were assigned tasks for the day. All male adults were given the arduous job of cutting down the trees. Due to the trees' height and the poor quality of their axes, the men had to take turns cutting down each tree. Once the tree fell, they had to dig around the stump as deep as possible to remove the root and fully eradicate the tree. Depending on the size of the trees, they could remove about five to ten trees per day. Meanwhile, the females were tasked with clearing weeds in sections of the mountain to make space for growing rice crops.

Every evening, the Khmer Rouge would play their music loudly in designated areas of the village and urged everyone to join. Many of the young people would gather for some form of entertainment, dancing in circles to the music. The song lyrics were focused on making the country safer and improving it in various ways.

A few days later, the appointed village leader and the traitors, as we called them, came to our home unexpectedly. They searched for all the valuable items, and they took the remaining valuables that we had. Our house was so small that there was no room to hide anything. Besides that, there was no warning whatsoever. They told us that we were not allowed to have or wear any kind of jewelry at all because since we were all equal, there would be no need for individuality. There was not much we could do so we just accepted and allowed them to take whatever they wanted. The Khmer Rouge knew well in their heart that these people whom they appointed to be our leaders would care less about how we felt after they took our belongings. They enjoyed watching our suffering. They took our belongings and gave them to their own families. The next day, I saw their daughter wear one of the gold necklaces that they took away from my mom. I was so furious, but I could not say anything.

One morning before we got ready to work, the Khmer Rouge held a meeting, and everyone needed to attend. The Khmer Rouge told us that from now on, all the children would belong to the authorities, not to our parents. Parents were allowed to give birth to the children and raise them until they were a certain age, but after that, the children belonged to the Ungaleer. Parents had no right to claim the children as their own. All parents were in shock after hearing that along with the children. They continued to tell us that our parents would stay behind in the village; the children would be the number forced to be in the front line to help the Ungaleer. They would take at least one child from each family to work wherever they wanted us to. We were frightened because they did not tell us what they wanted us to do or how far away we would be. All they said was that we would be taken away to wherever they decided to put us. They started to call each family name and instructed the parents to which child they wanted to have taken.

All the parents were in complete fear that their child was going to be called. My heart was about to jump out of my chest, and I just hoped that they would skip our family when they were reading down the list. Suddenly, I heard our last names called and then they called my older brother and me. My fear of being separated from my family resurfaced and I was in complete awe. I still remembered how frightened and lonely I was when I separated from my family the last time before the war ended. I had never thought that I had to go through that again, but I had no choice. There was nothing that anyone could do except to take the order. Before the meeting was over, they told us to prepare for the journey tomorrow morning. They gave us two cups of uncooked rice to take with us and told us to bring a small pot, a spoon, and a plate because we needed to cook on the way. For the remainder of the day, we were allowed to stay with our parents for the last time to prepare food and supplies.

There was nothing our parents could do except hope for the best and parked up whatever they could for the children. Because I was a girl, my parents worried a lot more about me than my brother. They knew that he could take care of himself, but I was younger, and I was just a young girl, so they just feared the worst for me. My mother prepared some food for me to take along and packed a small blanket for me. The whole night I was sleepless and thinking about what was going to happen to me and many other things starting from tomorrow.

8

Journey to The Labor Camp

The morning approached and my brother and I, along with forty-two other boys and girls met in part of the village. Parents were sad and said goodbye to their children because they had no idea where the authorities were going to take their children, and when they would see us again. My parents worried as well. They told me not to worry about them at home and to take care of myself. I knew they tried to be strong like many other parents, but deep down inside it was killing them to see us taken away from them, and they could not do anything about it. After proper goodbyes to our parents, the Khmer Rouge assigned one of the oldest girls and one of the oldest boys from the village to be our leader for the journey and then one female and one male Khmer Rouge led us and we followed them.

The journey began by walking out of the village. I felt so sad when I looked back to see my parents, brothers, and sisters wave goodbye to my brother and me. It was a goodbye without knowing when we would return if we were ever going to return. It was the goodbye that I did not want to happen, but it was happening, and I needed to do it. The goodbye wave was soon dismissed as we got farther from the village.

We had to walk through the rice farm before we reached the road. They said that this was the only way to get there and since none of us knew better, we listened and followed every word. Before we reached the road, we had to walk through the bumpy rice field for a few hours. One side of my sandals broke, I was struggling to walk with one side, and it slowed me down. After a while, the other side also broke, and I had to cope with walking around without them. Who knew we would all find ourselves in a situation like this. It felt like glass shards were piercing my skin with each step I took because of the rough edges of the field, and the uneven ground caused by flooding during rainy seasons. Trudging on for as long as I could, and even longer than I felt I could last, my foot hurt badly from all the blisters that surfaced on my foot. With every step I took, a blister popped and two more came out to replace it. I was in so much agony and I could not help feeling close to the end. There were so many instances that I felt I could not last any longer and my legs gave up on me. I was near the front at the time, so the Khmer Rouge did not notice me and people around me helped me up. After a while, I gained a little confidence and started the cycle all over again. I would start in the front, and then fall near the back of the crowd and have trouble trying to stay with everyone, and then I would rush back to the front because I knew when I fell, I would need some leverage to keep me with the group. I was so envious of everyone else because they all lived in the mountains and their feet were used to the ground. I could not complain because I knew that I would end up getting some type of cruel punishment and every step that I took I needed to remind myself that it was one less step to the end.

Besides the soreness in my foot, I was feeling hungry. When would the Khmer Rouge allow us to take a lunch break? I looked at the sun as I adapted the new way of telling time because we did not have any kind of watch to tell the time anymore. I started to recognize the approximate time of the day by looking at my own shadow. For example,

when the sun was about one step away on the right side that meant 1 pm

when the sun was about one step away to the left that meant 11 am when the sun was about two steps to the right that meant 2 pm

when the sun was about two steps to the left that meant 10 am

when the sun was as far as our tall, that meant 5 pm

when the sun was straight on top of us, we would stand on top of our shadow and knew that it was noon time.

These were the new ways that we learned to tell time. As far as the day of the week or what month of the year, we had no idea, we could only assume.

The shadow beneath me showed that it was already late in the afternoon. The hunger that had been gnawing at my stomach intensified, and I could see the same hunger reflected in the exhausted faces of those around me. We were all famished, but a deep sense of fear and caution prevented us from expressing our needs to the Khmer Rouge.

The cruel regime of the Khmer Rouge had inflicted unimaginable suffering upon us, and any signs of weakness or vulnerability were met with harsh consequences. We had learned to keep our hunger concealed, even as our bodies weakened, and our spirits faltered.

To our surprise, we noticed that even the Khmer Rouge soldiers seemed hungry. They appeared tired and irritable, a stark contrast to their usual stern and menacing demeanor. It was then that they ordered us to take a thirty-minute lunch break. During this break, however, we were expected to cook our meals within that limited timeframe.

Despite the offer of a brief respite, a sense of uncertainty lingered within me. I hesitated to use the food my mother had packed for me earlier that morning. It was a precious resource, and I couldn't predict what lay ahead of us on our arduous journey. The fear of an unknown future compelled me to reserve the food, preserving it for a time when it might be more desperately needed.

With caution and apprehension, we all gathered our meager supplies and quickly set about cooking our meager meals.

As the thirty minutes swiftly ticked away, some of us managed to put together whatever rations we could scrounge up.

The Khmer Rouge abruptly announced the end of our lunch break, some of us had not even finished cooking our meals. However, I considered myself fortunate, as my rice had just reached the perfect consistency in time. Hastily, I packed up my food along with a few others who were in a similar position, and we resumed our arduous journey.

Walking and eating simultaneously became the norm, as there was little time for respite. We shared our rice with those whose meals were not yet ready, understanding the shared struggle we faced. Despite the pain in my foot, which made each step a challenge, I pushed myself to walk as fast as I could, desperate not to fall too far behind.

Soon rain clouds began to appear and it started to drizzle. It only got harder, and we were forced to walk under the rain. There were no houses anywhere, and all we could do was continue to march in unison under the rain. As it got darker, we were cold, wet, and afraid. It was like a horror movie, there was a storm, and we were all miserable and terrified. The lightning and thunder only added to our macabre feelings toward life, and it was just so terrible. After a bolt of lightning hit the ground only a few meters away from us, we saw a shed and rushed to it. It was a sign of hope for us, and we all ran to it as fast as we could. The shed was not big, but it gave us enough room to fit everybody in it. We all were soaked and hungry. There was little to no food left over from this afternoon and everyone shared so we all had only a few bites to eat. It was so dark that the only way we could see each other was when there was lightning. Everyone, including the Khmer Rouge, fell asleep almost immediately.

It was early in the morning when we all woke up from my screams. I screamed because I felt something on my foot. When I looked at it, it was a worm that was crawling on my foot, I quickly wiped it off. I was not the only one that didn't like worms. Some others got up so fast to stay away from them.

The shed that we saw last night disappeared and it ended up being a large piece of wood propped on very thin pillars that looked as if they were about to collapse. There were two walls that a few people leaned on. As everyone woke up, we all saw worms crawling all around. Because it just rained, worms came out of the ground.

I was feeling stiff all over my body from the walk, and I did not want to walk for another day like that, but I had no choice. I forced myself very hard to get up and get ready, I was not the only one that felt like that. The Khmer Rouge noticed that and told us to move faster, it was time to continue the journey. We slept without dinner last night and there was no breakfast this morning, but there was nothing we could do, other than take the order. We were told that we would arrive at the destination in a matter of hours. It was next to impossible for me to walk because my old blisters cracked and there was nothing between my feet. The burning pavement along with all the pebbles that would seep into my foot awakened the hiding pain and I had to ignore it. I kept repeating to myself that it was all in my head and that I would be able to make it. I kept repeating to myself that it was all in my head and that I would be able to make it. I could not let anyone help me because if I could not support myself now, how was I going to last for events to come?

About an hour in, we all became hungry and were hoping that they would give us a break at any moment, but they didn't. Instead, they told us that it would not be much longer now and to wait for a bit longer before we would take a break. After another couple of hours, one brave soul asked, and the Khmer Rouge told us that the Ungaleer wanted us to arrive before the second day ended. They looked almost as scared as us when we asked, and that just made us even more terrified. If their Ungaleer installed this type of fear in their troops, what was going to happen to us if we made a mistake or if we did not work to their standards?

We could hear music as we got closer to the construction site. Again, the song's lyrics talked about working together, protecting our country, working hard to preserve its integrity, and so on. They wanted us to feel good about what they wanted to do for the county and us with the music. We could see hundreds of people waiting in line from a distance. They arrived earlier than we did and were already working. I got the impression that the area where we were going to work was once a forest as we got closer to it. Many trees were still left down on the ground and some of the tree stumps had not been removed. Many of the small size sheds were built from the trees and they were everywhere. It looked like many people had been camping here for a while. The smoke could also be seen from the different sheds. Each one had something different and the one that was closest to us was for cooking. I never saw so many people working together like that before and I just knew that for however long it lasted, it was going to be the hardest times in my life.

It didn't resemble anything we had done before, so I had no idea we would be operating in a forest. Every time I was taken to the jungle, we eventually turned it into a farm and grew things there, but this time that wasn't the case. The Khmer Rouge informed us that we would construct a road. For several miles, people carried a bamboo staff on their shoulders while attaching a basket to the end of it. When we passed by, we saw everyone's clothes were muddy and soaked. Girls were spread out over the labor site while all the boys worked in one area. It was forbidden for boys and girls to talk to one another. As soon as we got there, the male troop would direct the boys to the boys' job site, and the girls to the girls' job site. How we were going to construct this was all I could think about. Would we be completing this by hand? How long would it take to complete this? Would I ever see my family again?

The Khmer Rouge troops then led us to the spot where they wanted us to stay. It was in the so-called "excavated" part of the jungle where most of the trees were cut down. There was nothing here except a few stumps here and there. There were no sheds built here so all we had was the ground that we were going to sleep on and the sky to look at as our roof.

By the time we had gotten there and put all our bags down, it was late afternoon. Since we walked the past two days without rest, I thought that we would have at least the rest of the day off, but I was wrong. As soon as we received our designated area, we were told to get a hoe, 2 baskets, and a long bamboo stick from the troops and get to work right away.

9

Cook for a Large Group- and Sleeping Under The Rain

My foot was swollen and became covered in blisters and blood because of the two days of walking barefoot. It felt agonizing just looking at it. Desperately seeking some compassion, I showed my foot to one of the female Khmer Rouge members, hoping she would understand and allow me to rest. Instead, to my dismay, she called me a "spoiled brat." She emphasized that everyone else had to endure the same walking and continue working, making it clear that I would not be an exception to the demanding circumstances.

Persistently attempting to reason with her, she looked at my foot again, and eventually, she relented, but she told me I had to cook for the others who had to work. She guided me to one of the sheds with a few other troops inside. They all looked excited to see me and started asking me about my cooking skills and then handed me some uncooked rice and fermented fish to prepare dinner for my villagers.

I was nervous and apprehensive because I had never cooked for that many people before. My cooking experience was limited to occasionally cooking for my siblings. It was crucial for me to ensure that dinner was ready by the time everyone returned from work, as any delay or inconvenience could potentially lead to trouble.

I began searching for some dried wood and three large stones to create a triangle stove. This setup would allow me to place a cooking pot on top and create a fire underneath. However, I faced a challenge, I had nothing to ignite the fire. Observing others nearby, I noticed they were also cooking not far from me. I approached them politely and asked if they could spare some fire to help me to start on my own. Generously, they offered me a piece of their burning wood. I saw them cooking with a big pot like the one that I had received from the troops. I asked how to cook with such a large pot, and they kindly explained the step-by-step process to me.

It was not hard at all to start the fire with burning wood. I started to boil the water, added the uncooked rice to the pot, and closed the lid. I waited for about 5 minutes or so for it to completely boil again and then poured the excess water out closed the lid and reduced the flame to low. The rice started to cook slowly with a low flame. About twenty minutes later, my rice was ready. I was filled with a mixture of relief and excitement as I managed to cook 20 cups of rice all at once. Since the pot was not big enough to cook at one time for everyone, I had to pour the already-cooked rice out so that I could use the pot to cook again. But there was not anything for me to pour the rice into. I went to the woods and picked some of the biggest leaves that I could find. I connected those leaves with small sticks to make it like a big sheet, and then I poured the cooked rice over it. Then I continued to cook another pot of rice. After I had cooked enough rice for everyone, I cooked fermented fish in a smaller pot for people to eat with rice. By the end of the day, I was exhausted from all the cooking. But I was so happy as well that I was able to cook for so many people, which I had never thought that I could do.

Now that the food was ready, I was able to relax a little. I realized that during the period I was cooking, the anxiety made me completely forget about my foot. I was lying down on the ground feeling relief from the anxiety for the past two days. The sky was getting darker, and people had not gotten out of work yet. My foot felt a little better since I did not have to work in the muddy environment and walk back and forth transporting dirt from one place to another.

I was about to fall asleep when I heard the noise from the people who got out of work. I got up and saw hundreds of people walking in line toward their shelter. Each one of them carried a hoe and a long bamboo stick, which had one basket hanging on each side. And then I saw our group carrying the same thing as hundreds of others, their clothes were all dirty with mud, and they all looked tired and hungry. They were just so happy to see that food was ready for them. They did not bother to clean themselves up first; they went to their bags took out their plates and spoons and went straight to the food.

At this time, they would enjoy eating anything that they could have. The rice with fermented fish was delicious, but not for me, not now. Since I was not used to eating that, and I did not like the scent of it, I got a bowl of rice with a few pieces of rock salt and ate far away from the others. Rice with salt was so boring and had no flavor besides saltiness. Then I remembered my mom packed some food for me before I left home. I got up to check my bag and found a bag of food wrapped in a banana leaf. I was so happy to see that and took it out of my bag. I walked back to where I sat early by myself and opened it and saw what was inside the wrapper. I was so glad to see that it was my favorite food. It was fish sauteed with lemongrass, tamarind, and spices, then wrapped with banana leaf and toasted. The smell was so good; I took one small piece and chewed it slowly. It was so delicious, and I wanted to enjoy every bite of it because when all this food was gone, I did not know when I could eat that again. Then I heard the voice ask me "What do you have, it smells good! Can I have some?". Before I got a chance to answer, one of my groups came to sit next to me and got a piece of my mom's cooking. "Um," the sound that she made got the others' attention. Before I got a chance to take my second piece, everyone was around me and tried to reach into my food as well.

Then all I saw was a banana leaf; the food that was wrapped in it was gone. All I heard was the complement of the food. They wanted to know who made it and what was in it. I did not know what else to say except smile and told them that was my mom's cooking, and I did not know exactly what was in it besides lemongrass and tamarind. That was the only food that I was able to eat with my rice at the time. Now that I did not have it anymore, I returned to eating rice with salt and as for the others, they resumed their fermented fish.

Fermented fish, a culinary ingredient that elicited mixed reactions, was known to impart a unique flavor and enhance the taste of a variety of dishes when used in cooking.

Normally used for cooking to make food more delicious. While some find it delectable and enjoyable, others may have different preferences and opinions about its distinct taste and aroma.

After we had our dinner, everyone cleaned their plate and put it back into their backpack. Then they searched for the best spot on the ground as their bed and got right to sleep. As for me I started cleaning up the pots and had them ready for the next day. Due to our exhaustion from work, we fell asleep as soon as our backs hit the ground.

We were abruptly awakened by the Khmer Rouge, signaling that it was time to rise and prepare ourselves for another day of work. It felt as if we just fell asleep, and it was time to get up already. I glanced at the sky; it was still shrouded in darkness with no sign of the sun impending rising. Since there was no clock to tell the time, I assumed that it was about four or five am. Our bodies were fatigued from the previous day's labor, and all stiff and did not feel like waking up at all, but we did not have any choice.

I, too, reluctantly pulled myself from sleep, though my destination differed from the rest. I looked at everyone and tried very hard to get up and gather what was needed for another day of building roadways. They were all half asleep when they gathered their tools and walked in the line toward the work site. As for me, I did not want to waste any time, so even though it was still dark; I started to do whatever I could to prepare lunch. By the time my lunch was ready, it was still too early for people to get out for lunch. Then I went off to the nearby woods, gathering branches, and started to construct a temporary shelter.

Building a shelter single-handedly proved to be a challenging task, but I was resolute in my determination to make it happen. Day after day, I would seize the opportunity before lunchtime to gather a few tree branches, gradually accumulating the material needed. With each passing day, my progress became evident as I successfully put up four sturdy tree branches as the main poles for our shelter. Utilizing smaller branches adorned with leaves, I was able to intertwine them to use as the roof and the walls. Upon completing the construction, I stood there for a while to look at the shelter that I just built, and I was so proud of myself for my accomplishment. As time passed, I felt more confident that I could do anything if I put my effort into it.

The shelter I built proved to be an asset for our group. During the scorching daytime heat, we enjoyed our lunch under the shed instead of under the sun, and at night it kept the moisture away from us while we slept. Thankfully, we had not encountered any rainy days since our arrival, and the shelter had yet to be put to the test again for nature's shower.

Just like any other night, we were deeply asleep, but this night relentless rain started to pour on us with great intensity. The shelter I built was only good to shield the sun, not the rain. We were getting wet from the water seeping through the leak of the roof and the wall. Initially, we all tried to sit up, hoping the rain would go away soon, allowing us to return to our sleep. We sat and leaned on each other for comfort. We waited and waited for the rain to go away. It had been an hour already and the rain was still going strong. Some of us started to fall asleep while sitting down. Then one after another we were all asleep and instead of sitting down, we slowly leaned to the ground. Our resting spot was situated slightly on the hillside; therefore, we felt the rain run through our backs. Despite the discomfort, we did not care to get up because we were so tired.

It rained for the whole night, and we did not have much sleep. It kept most of us awake, soaking, and discomforted. We hoped that the circumstances would exempt us from the day's work, considering the heavy rain. However, the Khmer Rouge remained unaffected by the weather conditions. Rain or shine, it had no significance to them. Their shelter, constructed with solid materials such as wood and metal sheets, provided them with a dry and comfortable place to sleep.

As everyone was on their way to work, I started to take care of everyone's wet clothes, ensuring they would have dry garments to wear. Then I started to prepare food for other days ahead. It was a nightmare to start a fire after the rain. I kept blowing and blowing to make the wood stay burning until my eyes were red because of the smoke. It was not easy due to the wet ground and wet woods. It took me about two hours to finally manage to keep the wood burning. I was concerned that my food would not be ready in time. It was very difficult, but I managed to get food ready just in time for lunch.

During our two-month stay at the job site, our daily food supply remained unchanged: rice, fermented fish, and salt. I thought that for a period, I would have grown accustomed to this diet, but I still had problems adjusting myself to this. The girls in my group had tried to convince me that it was delicious and urged me to give it a chance. they claimed I would love it, but I remained unconvinced.

I was fortunate that sometimes, the girls brought back some food such as snails and crabs they found while digging the ground at work, and shared them with me. I put them over the fire, and it was delicious.

The job site stretched out like an endless small Mountain range, interconnected to one another. During our lunch break, a female Khmer Rouge approached our shelter with exciting news. She informed us that the road construction was nearly complete, and as a result, not everyone needed to be here anymore. A certain group would remain to finish the job, while the rest of us would be allowed to return home to our parents. The announcement filled us with huge joy and relief. Finally, after all this time, we would have the opportunity to reunite with our loved ones.

However, along with the relief came a wave of terror and horror. We discovered that a few individuals who had gone missing were victims of the Khmer Rouge. They had been brutally killed and their bodies buried beneath the road we had constructed. It was a chilling revelation that shook us to our core. We came to realize that this was a twisted ritual carried out after the completion of each major construction project. The knowledge of this sinister act cast a dark shadow over our joy and filled us with deep sorrow and apprehension.

The journey to the new location took a whole day of walking through unforgiving terrain. When we finally arrived, we found ourselves in another dense jungle, much like the previous site. There were some people already there. Our hopes of returning home were shattered as we were abruptly redirected to another labor camp. We made our way to the shelter controlled by the Khmer Rouge to get food. They gave us just enough water to cook our meals and a ration of rice. We were sternly informed that water was short in supply and that we must use it sparingly. The scarcity of resources only added to the hardship we faced in this new environment.

It was indeed an unbearable situation to be expected to work without enough water supply. When we questioned the authorities about this, they informed us that we had to walk for two hours to reach the water source. This meant that obtaining water became yet another challenge in our daily struggle. With limited water available, our meals were affected, and after eating, there was little water left for drinking. This scarcity of water had a domino effect on our hygiene as well. We could not clean ourselves or brush our teeth properly due to the lack of water. Even washing our dishes became a luxury, as our water was portioned to just a few tablespoons per person. Consequently, we could only dust off the dishes and put them away without cleaning. It was a harsh reality that further compounded the difficulties we faced at the construction site.

The task of chopping down trees and getting rid of stumps to make room for the road was physically demanding, especially considering the lack of water available. We were left with no choice but to dig in search of springs that could provide us with water.

Our efforts, dig after dig, however, yield no water. We discovered that some areas contained water, but it was not drinkable because it was filthy, cloudy, and odorless. To purify such water, we resorted to using salt. While the addition of salt helped with clearing the water, it was still unsuitable for use as it retained a distinct salty taste and smell. It was disheartening to face yet another obstacle in our quest for clean and drinkable water.

I was put in charge of acquiring sufficient water for a group. However, we faced challenges due to the lack of suitable buckets or containers. It was a difficult task to transport the water without spilling too much along the way. Determined to find a solution, I observed others and learned the techniques of using a vine to create a rope and a tree branch to create a yoke to carry more water. Despite my efforts, the journey to the water source was exhausting, and upon reaching a nearby pond, I took a short rest before filling up a few pots with water, ensuring to cover them tightly. I covered myself with water so I could keep myself cool on the trip back. Unfortunately, by the time I arrived back at the camp, a third of the water had spilled, leaving me frustrated with tedious tasks that yielded little result.

I had to find a way to manage my time more intently and I needed to approach the water fetching trip with greater focus. This time, I used a new technique by placing leaves on top of a pot filled with water. The leaves acted as a protective layer. reducing the chance of spills during transport. Compared to my previous attempt, I was able to successfully keep most of the water in place.

We'd been at the new site for a few weeks now, and there hadn't been a single drop of rain. In a way, this lack of rain turned out to be somewhat beneficial since we did not have proper shelter. Our "bed" was bare ground, and our "roof" was the open sky above us.

One day, the Khmer Rouge drove a cow wagon carrying a big barrel full of water to our work site. We were so excited to see that. The water provided was strictly for cooking and drinking purposes, and we were warned not to use it for anything else.

We waited in line patiently to get our share of water. However, despite having access to water, we could not wash our plates after eating as it was prohibited. Later that evening, I witnessed a female Khmer Rouge member washing her feet with water. It was distracting and frustrating to witness such a contradiction. We were not allowed to wash our plates after eating, yet they had the privilege of using water to clean their feet. It seemed like the rule applied differently to us compared to them.

Although the arrival of the water was a moment of relief, it also meant that those responsible for collecting water, including myself, had to resume our work duties.

A few days later, we received the unexpected news that our group, along with another, was granted permission to return home. The joyfulness and relief we felt were indescribable. The following morning, we proceeded on our journey home, filled with anticipation and happiness. As we were on our way, we stumbled upon a pond of water. Overwhelming by the sight, we dropped our belongings and hurriedly ran towards the pond, desperate for a chance to clean ourselves. With a mix of exhaustion and excitement, we submerged ourselves in the water, washing away the grimness and weariness accumulated over the past few weeks. It was a refreshing and rejuvenating experience, restoring a sense of cleanliness and dignity.

As the sun began to set, we finally arrived at a small town along the way. The authorities allowed us to stay there for the night, providing some rest and shelter.

Indeed, it was the first time since we left home that we had a proper roof over our heads. This simple shelter provided by the small town gave us the sense of security and comfort that we had longed for. As we settled in for the night, we could not help but offer a semblance of privacy. It was a small yet significant reminder of the normalcy we had left, and we yearned to return to.

1 0

Making A Major Decision

The next morning two of the female Khmer Rouge came and informed us that they would lead the way. It was an exciting day for all of us, as we were finally able to return home and reunite with our parents, brothers, and sisters. Our journey back home was overwhelming. We had more energy than ever, and we walked as fast as we could, eager to reach our destination.

We walked about half a day when we arrived at Preah Netr Preah, the town where my family and nine other families resided before the Khmer Rouge separated us. Upon our arrival, there were thousands of people like us gathered there.

The Khmer Rouge guided us to one of the vacated homes in town and told us it would be our temporary place to stay. Eager to know when we could finally return home, we asked. They instructed us to get ready for the meeting, and that we would receive further information.

Later, at the meeting, The Khmer Rouge told us that we were not allowed to go home until our jobs were finished, and they would let us know when that happened. As soon as we heard the news, our hope of going home vanished. We knew that the Khmer Rouge never told us the truth. All they did was trick us one time after another, and we could not do anything about it. If we waited for them to tell us we could go home, it would probably never happen. They continued telling us that we were all part of an organization called "Ungaleer," which would be responsible for providing us with food and shelter instead of our parents. They tried to convince us that by registering to become members of Ungaleer, we would receive improved provisions and accommodations. They assured us that we would be assigned various roles within different departments, such as doctors, clothes makers, soldiers, and so on. Their preservative words aimed to immerse us into accepting this new system and embracing the opportunity they claimed it would bring.

They were the people who would lead the country and would make the country stronger, with more power, more food, and more clothing than ever before. They claimed that if we worked hard, over the period of seven years we would have anything we wanted. We would be able to wear any color of clothing and would have all kinds of food to eat.

They would give us two weeks to think about and make decisions. In the meantime, they'd give us half a cup of uncooked rice per day for each person. They told us that within two weeks of decision-making, we did not have to work, and we should not waste our food.

Two weeks of waiting with a half cup of uncooked rice per day for each person was not enough. We had to find an alternative food to add to what they gave us so that we would not be feeling too hungry all day long. Many people would just pick any wild berries or any kind of weeds that they thought would be edible. Most of us could not tell if the berries or the weeds were poisonous or not.

Due to hunger, some people would not care about the risks of what they eat. The red and juicy wild fruits looked delicious. The results of eating those berries were scary as well. It did not take long, just a matter of minutes after eating; the people who ate the wild berries were vomiting and collapsed one after another. It was frightening to witness all this tragedy in front of us, and all of these were caused by hunger. Due to the high number of people poisoned from eating the berries, the Khmer Rouge brought in two big trucks and took them to the hospital. That's what they said, but did the hospital even exist?

Having witnessed several hundreds of people collapse after consuming poisonous wild berries, many people made their decision to register to become a part of the Khmer Rouge. Many thoughts came to mind; when would we return home, would we ever have decent food? Would they ever allow us to have enough to eat? Joining them now might provide us with enough food, but waiting would not.

I believed that was the Khmer Rouge's intention, to play with our minds. and it worked like magic. The next day, the Khmer Rouge set up a table on the sidewalk for people to volunteer. In the early morning of that day, there were only a few people that were signing up. And then as time went by, more and more people were standing in line waiting for a turn to register.

I was feeling sad to see some girls from the same village as me signing up one after another along with hundreds of other people. They all hoped that they would have better lives if they were one of them. The Khmer Rouge ordered all the people who registered to take their belongings and to stay together in a group because the truck would come to pick them up in a couple of days. As days went by, more and more people were registered, and it seemed like there were more boys and girls.

98

Soon, one-third of the people were signed up and prepared to be picked up. As for the girls from my village, there were only six of us left who refused to register. We promised each other that it did not matter what happened, we would never volunteer to register to become one of them. At this point, I must hang on to the other five girls who came from the same village. I was scared and confused about the direction, and I did not have a clue which way the village where my parents lived was. If the Khmer Rouge would allow me to go back home by myself, I had no idea which way I should start to walk and if I could ever make it home.

Then, the big day for the people that signed up had arrived. Three big trucks came to town to pick them up. Most of them seemed very excited while others seemed like they were not sure they had made the right decision. We watched them get on the truck and wondered where the Khmer Rouge took them. Would they have better food and better shelter as the Khmer Rouge said? Those were some of the questions we had, and we would never get any answers.

Several hours later, the town was much quieter because about half of the people were gone. The five girls and I were worried because we did not know what would happen to us next. We promised each other that we must stay together wherever we go.

Just a couple of hours later, the Khmer Rouge called for a meeting. They did not waste any time at all, they told us to prepare for work in the morning and we would be working in the rice field to separate the rice crop and replant them.

Work with the rice crop? It did not sound like difficult work at all. I could do it. After walking two days without shoes while my feet were blistering, sleeping under the rain while worms crawled on my feet, and cooking for large numbers of people, there was nothing else that I could not do. I must constantly remind myself of it.

As thoughts went through my mind, I heard the Khmer Rouge announce that they would arrange every ten people as one group. As soon as I heard that, I awakened from my thoughts and whispered to the other girls that we must not separate from each other. We would sit as close to each other as quickly as we could before the Khmer Rouge separated us. But there were just six of us; we were not enough to make up a full group. We were frightened that the Khmer Rouge would pick any one or more of us to make a group with the other people.

We were not the only group that was afraid to be separated from the people we knew. Many others were in the same situation just like us; they tried to hang on to each other as quickly as they could to avoid being called by the Khmer Rouge. Everyone seemed afraid of separating from the people they knew. After all that, what we had left were the people from the same village and we must do whatever we could to stay together.

The whispering, getting up, and trying to stay in a group were disturbing the Khmer Rouge. One of them pointed his gun in the air and fired. The sound of the gunshot was frightening to us; we quickly sat down and stayed quiet. The Khmer Rouge told us that there was nothing to worry about, they were not going to kill us, and we shouldn't panic. All they wanted us to do was to arrange ourselves in a group of ten people so they would know how many people were remaining. We felt a little relieved but still did not want to be separated from the people we knew.

All of us were sitting in the group, but there were not many groups that consisted of ten people the way the Khmer Rouge wanted. My group was one of the groups that was short four people. The Khmer Rouge then arranged each group to ten. The people who were separated from their group were sad and scared, but they had to obey the orders they were given by the Khmer Rouge to get up from their group and join other groups.

We were lucky that we managed to stay together as a group. The Khmer Rouge appointed four people to join us to make it one group. After we were all in a group of ten people, the Khmer Rouge combined three groups into one which consisted of thirty people. They assigned one of their people to be our leader and to watch over us. Boys would have a male Khmer Rouge as the group leader and girls would have a female Khmer Rouge as the group leader. We were not allowed to have any kind of communication at all between boys and girls, even though we were brothers and sisters. Since the day we arrived at Preanateprea, I had not seen my brother yet.

1 1

The Fear of Leeches in the Rice Field

T he next morning as early as about five A.M. we were woken up by the Khmer Rouge to get ready to go to work. We walked in a line on the road toward the job site. There was a long line of people, and I could not tell how many were remaining, but there were several hundred of us. Boys walked on one side of the road and girls walked on the other side. While we walked, I kept looking across from the road hoping to see my brother walking in line with hundreds of others. Until now, I had not seen my brother at all since the day we arrived from building the roadway. I knew that he did not register to become one of the communist Khmer Rouge because I was watching those people get on the truck and I did not see him. Perhaps I may have missed seeing him and he did get on the truck along with hundreds of others. Anyway, there was nothing much I could do besides hoping that he was fine and somehow, I could spot him somewhere, someday soon, so that I would know for sure that he was all right as well.

It took us about one hour to arrive at the work site not too far away from the road. We left the road and made our way towards the rice field that stretched for miles. It was covered in water that was about one to two feet deep. The field had been divided into many smaller sections with the walls built from dirt or land. These walls were approximately five feet high from the water and they were about one to two feet wide. The purpose of it was to collect water, plant rice crops, and provide just enough room for us to walk on to reach different parts of the rice field.

The morning sun was still a bit dim and dreary when we arrived at the rice field. It was my first time learning how the rice crops were grown. The process started by loosening up the hardened ground using a special tractor that could drive in the mud. Alternatively, cows could pull the ground separator to achieve the same result. The soil was then added to fertilize the ground and help the rice seeds grow better, thicker, and greener. When the rice crops grew to about a foot, it was time to pull them out from the ground and replant them in the muddy field, ideally spaced about six inches apart. Our job for the day was to replant the rice crops in the muddy water.

For the first time in my life, as well as for hundreds of others, we were ordered to work in the murky water. The muddy field was repulsive and unpleasant to work in, but the real horror came from the slimy black creatures that lived there: leeches. These shiny, wriggling things ranged in size from as tiny as a toothpick to as big as a thumb and swam all around us. These creatures lived in this kind of shadowy muddy water that does not move. We were instructed to plant the rice crops, but the thought of these creatures attaching themselves to our legs and sucking our blood terrified us. As soon as we put our feet in the water, the leeches would swim to us as fast as they could, latch onto our legs, and bite into our skin. We would scream in terror and quickly run back to the land. As a result, we ended up pacing back and forth on top of the small wall, too scared to step into the water and do our job.

An hour had passed, and we were still hesitant to step into the water. We stood on the land, too afraid of the leeches that infested the muddy field. Not far away from the work site, a few female Khmer Rouges watched us screaming from the side of the road. It was too far for them to tell us what to do and they did not want to come to the field. Instead, they yelled at us to get into the field and start working. We had to muster the courage to step into the water, but it was so frightening that we could only stay in the field for a few minutes at a time before running back to the land. The Khmer Rouge grew impatient with us and one of them fired a warning shot into the air, to warn us that if we did not want to get into any kind of trouble, we must go in the field and work like nothing was bothering us. We had to do whatever we could to overcome the fear of the leeches. It was easier said than done. Only a few of us were not afraid, and when the leeches attached themselves to our skin, we would call for help instead of running back to the land. We managed to work until lunchtime, but not much progress was made. It felt more like we were dancing in the muddy field than planting rice crops.

Most of us were feeling uneasy and afraid of the leeches after witnessing how they could attach to our skin. After lunch, we had to come up with a solution to protect ourselves from these creatures. We used a vine to tie our pant legs tightly so that the leeches could not hang on to our skin. We buried our feet in the mud to prevent the leeches from finding a way into our pants and biting our skin. The plan was somewhat successful, as the leeches swam around us but could not bite our skin. However, we had to work quickly with our hands when planting the rice crops in the muddy water. we had to pull our hands back quickly so that those leeches did not get a chance to hang onto our hands and at the same time speed up our work. Although the leeches still managed to hang onto our clothes, it was not as frightening as having them attached to our skin, but it still looked creepy. Eventually, the day passed.

That first night, I was abruptly awakened by a terrifying dream. In my dream, I found myself in a vast rice field, but to my horror, countless leeches were clinging to my skin. Overwhelming with fear, I cried out for help, my screams echoing through the darkness.

It was over thirty degrees Celsius (90+ degrees F) every day. We had to walk from the rice field to the road to have our lunch. It took us at least ten minutes to get to the road. We only had thirty minutes for lunch each day. They only fed us just enough to survive and have the energy to work. We had to eat fast so that we could have some time to rest. I had to adapt to the situation which meant I had to learn to eat fast if I wanted to have some time to rest. Because of this, I ate my lunch fast. Then I soaked my scarf with water. I took about a five-minute nap on the side of the road. I covered myself with that wet scarf to keep myself cool.

As days went by, we got used to it. A few people who weren't afraid of the leeches helped pull them out from anyone who had gotten bitten by them. Some leeches were so hard to pull off because they hung on to our skin so tight with their tiny teeth and would not let go. We were so mad at those hideous, blood-sucking creatures. My fear of those creatures slowly faded away. And sometimes, I had enough courage to pull it out from my leg without help. But I still despised it very much.

An odd thing that we had to do was stick the leeches on a stick and stick them to the ground so that they couldn't move or hurt anyone. But sometimes, they would find a way to squirm out and come back.

Another experiment we tried was cutting them in half (I know, a little disgusting), and hoping that they would die, but they weren't too easy to kill. If we cut them in half, the two parts would just grow back and there would be two leeches instead of one. These creatures were impossible to get rid of. They multiplied extremely fast like ticks. We even tried to put them on a stick and burn them. And yes, we were that desperate to get rid of them.

Two months later, miles of the field were full of rice crops. The Khmer Rouge told us that as soon as we finished our work here, we would be able to return home. We were so happy to hear that we finally could go home to see our family. It had been almost a year that we were away from them. When we thought about going home, it gave us so much hope and energy to get up every morning and get ready to work, we worked as hard as we could.

Then one day before lunchtime, a few of the Khmer Rouge came to the work field. They announced that Ungar Leer needed our help to build a levee so that we could reserve rainwater and that we would be able to have enough water to grow rice crops four times a year instead of once a year, "we would have plenty of rice for everyone to eat and we could eat whenever we wanted to". We looked at each other speechless, they wanted us to build levees to save rainwater. There was plenty of rice before. Now that they controlled the country, we never had enough rice to eat anymore. What happened to all the rice? We could only guess but were afraid to express our thoughts or to say anything. If we said the wrong things our lives could be in danger. Did this mean that we would not be able to go home? The Khmer Rouge said that the rice field was almost finished and that they only kept some people to finish; the remainder of the people would go back to the camp to start packing our bags for the next adventure.

They started to call names that would stay. My heart was pounding and hoped that my name and the girls in my group would be called so that we could stay together. One name after another was called and finally, all the names were called. I did not hear my name or the girls in my group. I was so sad that I knew for sure that I would not be able to go home. At least not any time soon, but at the same time, I feel relief that our group was not separated. If I was separated from my group, I would get lost very easily in the direction of which way to go home. They had moved us so many times; that I had no idea where I was anymore. If the Khmer Rouge told me to go home, I had no clue which way I should walk to get home. That's how lost I was.

1 2

Building Levees by Hands

We arrived at the camp and started gathering our belongings. It did not take us long because we did not have much to pack anyway. We were allowed to have an early lunch before we began our journey.

It took us about four or five hours to walk to the new job site. It was near the side of the road. I only saw a shed that was supposed to be for the Khmer Rouge themselves, a place for storing food, and a big pile of hoes. This was not the first time that we had to sleep on the ground. The sky would be our roof and the ground would be our bed. We were told to stay together as a group of ten people and each group had to report to the Khmer Rouge in the shed to get food.

After our typical dinner of rice and fermented fish, which I finally was able to eat, we were called for a meeting. Each one of us was assigned to one of the hoes and a yoke which we must guard with our lives. They also assigned one of themselves to be our group leader. My group leader was a female Khmer Rouge named Chan. She looked a couple of years older than me.

The next morning at about 5 am, it was still dark and cool. We had to report to the work location. We did not have to walk too far to go to work; it was near the roadside where we slept. I wondered how we could build a levee in the water stream about three feet deep with our hands and a hoe. We were supposed to build it to hold the water. It did not matter to them; we had to get inside the water and start digging. We got into the water, and they put us in line about 20 feet away from the roadside. It was impossible to dig the mud out from inside three feet deep of water and put it in line to build a levee in the moving water stream. Three hours later, it was going nowhere, and we were cold. We had to keep our bodies inside the water so that we wouldn't feel too cold. As soon as we put a big piece of mud in the spot, the water stream would wash away. Nobody would say anything.

Two weeks passed by, and we still had to work in the water stream which seemed helpless. But the Ugar Lear did not allow us to stop. They told us that it did not matter how long it would take, the levee must be completed. In the meantime, our food supply had been cut low. We were not allowed to eat steamed rice anymore. We must cook with extra water to make up the volume of the food. Therefore, the food that we ate had more water. It would make us get hungry sooner. As we worked in the water, we always collected whatever we could for our diet such as small fish, snails, crabs, or any living things that we thought were edible.

One evening after work, Chan came to me and told me that she had gone through my bag while I was at work. She found my blouse and she liked it very much and asked if she could have it. Without any delay, I said yes. What else could I say? If I told her no, she might have gotten upset with me and I would be in trouble, or she'd just take it anyway. That blouse was important to me because it was the first piece of clothing that I had learned to make. I had it with me since I left my hometown in Mongkol Borey.

After I gave that blouse to her, she was so excited and joyful. Then, she gave me one of her black Khmer Rouge uniforms. It was a typical black, long-sleeved shirt. At that time no one had a black shirt unless you were one of the Khmer Rouge, so I took that shirt from her. She became friendlier and told me that I did not have to go to work in the water. I could stay on dry land and cook for my group.

My sacrifices had finally paid off. She loved my blouse and wore that under her black uniform all the time. It seemed to me like either she never had a blouse or that she just missed the colorful clothing. I felt bad for her, so I decided to use one of my clothes that I was not allowed to wear because it was floral fabric. I made a bra for her from that, and she was so thrilled.

As time passed, our friendship flourished and she confided in me, sharing things she had never revealed before. One of her deepest secrets was her inability to read or write, fearing judgment and ridicule from other members of the Khmer Rouge. She had been recruited into the organization at a young age and was indoctrinated to believe that education was unnecessary, dismissing it as a waste of time for lazy individuals. The Khmer Rouge propagated the idea that everyone would be treated the same, regardless of age, gender, or educational background. Although she gained insight into the inner workings of the group as a soldier, she felt powerless to change anything, knowing that resistance could lead to fatal consequences.

After a few weeks of cooking for my group, I noticed that other groups had better food than us. They had vegetables and fruits such as mango to share. I went to talk to them and learned that their group had assigned someone to the village that was close by to ask for fruit and vegetables from the villagers.

The ideas took hold of me; I realized that if I could go to see my parents and at the same time bring some food back from the village, it would be a tremendous help for my group. Then I decided to talk to my group leader and asked her permission to go to the village where my parents lived to find some food. To my surprise, she granted me permission for my journey.

Realizing that I did not know the route to the village, I felt a sense of unease. However, among my group, there was one girl that I could trust about direction. Being the oldest in the group, she was originally from the village where my parents lived. Her name was Yeam and she was a few years older than me. I approached my group leader and requested permission to bring Yeam along as my companion, both for guidance and assistance in carrying the provision back. Thankfully, my leader granted my request, understanding the importance of having someone familiar with the village by my side.

Everyone in the group asked me to take them because they all wanted to go home to see their parents. It was hard for me; I wish I could take them all. I knew how much we all wanted to go home to see our family. Since my leader agreed for me to take one person alone, I had to choose the person that I knew would lead us home, and that was Yeam.

My leader took out a notebook and a pencil from her backpack. Since she could not read or write, she told me to write myself a permission slip for travel. Because there would be Khmer Rouge soldiers guarding the road so that no one would dare to try to escape or go places without permission. She then asked me to read it back to her. She seemed overwhelmed and listened to what I wrote and asked me that when I returned from my trip, she wanted me to secretly teach her how to read and write. She also told me if the guard asked who wrote the note, I should inform them it was her. I agreed.

I was taken aback by the realization that most of the people in my group were illiterate with only a basic understanding of the alphabet and a few simple words. They asked me with heartfelt requests to write letters to their parents, conveying their thoughts and emotions. I asked permission from my leader; she kindly lent me her notebook and pencil for this purpose. That evening, I was busy writing individual letters for each person, capturing their words and sentiments as best as I could. The anticipation of delivering these messages filled me with excitement, making it difficult for me to find sleep that night.

The following morning while everyone was on their way to work, Yeam and I were on our journey to the village of

Phnom Sress. As my leader told me, on our way we encountered Khmer Rouge guards. They asked all kinds of questions such as, who our leader was, where were we going, and for what purpose. I presented them with the permission note. One of the guards took the note from me and showed it to the other guard. They examined it carefully while exchanging hushed whispers. They glanced at the note and whispered to each other. One of them asked me to read the note out loud. They seemed to know my group leader. They confirmed that it was indeed written by Chan. Satisfied with their investigation, they opened the gate, permitting us to proceed on our way.

1 3

Going Home to Phnom Sress

fter a half day of walking, we were tired and hungry. Because we had the permission slip, we were able to ask for food from one of the Khmer Rouge troop stations. We continued our journey for a few more hours when I saw the mountain from a distance. I asked Yarm "Is that our home there?" she said yes. I was surprised, I was not that far from home. Then she said we would need a boat to get home because this was the time of year when water was everywhere, and that we would need a boat to travel from place to place. I was wondering how we were going to find a boat. Yeam also had no idea since the Khmer Rouge took everything from people.

Shortly after that, we got closer to the water. I could see water everywhere just like the ocean. A few boats were being rowed in different directions depending on where their destination was. When I saw a boat arriving, I began asking how they acquired it. They said that anyone could use it if it was available because these boats belonged to the Khmer Rouge. A few more boats arrived but other people were there before us, so they got to use it first.

Finally, it was our turn, I could not wait to get home. Even though I grew up by the river, I never rowed a boat before. It was my first time traveling by boat and I had to learn how to row. Yeam showed me how to row a boat. Every year, she had to use the boat during the high tide season for traveling. It was not hard at all; it took me no time and I got it right away. I was so excited that I rowed as fast as I could so that I could get home soon.

It took us about an hour or so to get to Phnom Sress. After we docked the boat at the side of the mountain, we started to walk into the village. I would have gotten lost already if I did not have Yeam with me. There were so many kinds of fruit farms around the mountainside. We had to walk through a banana, mango, and orange farm and many others before we got into where our parents lived.

After we arrived at the village, I started to recognize and remember the way to walk home. Yeam's home was closer than mine, she got to her house before me. I told her that she had to ask her parents to help get some food to take back and that I would do the same. This way we were sure that we would have it. I made a quick stop at her house because Yeam wanted me to meet her parents. After she described how we came back to take food back to our group, her parents were so thankful to me that I brought their daughter along. She invited me to stay for dinner where they had sweet potatoes. At this moment the village was short of rice, so people were eating potatoes. I informed her that I needed to first go home. She told me not to forget to come for dinner.

I was so excited to go home that I ran as fast as I could. When I arrived, I saw a skinny person with no hair from behind standing on the side of the house doing some chores. I wondered who that person was. When I got closer, that person turned, she was my mom. I called her and started to cry right away. She looked at me in shock. My mom was strong with short hair, and she was a healthy-looking woman before I left for the labor camps. But when I saw that she was skinny and had a bald head, I was shocked to see her look like that. I cried, my mom cried, and my dad heard a crying noise, he came out and saw me, he was surprised as well. They did not expect me to show up in front of them. It was over a year after I left. After we all calmed down from crying, my parents wanted to know everything that I had gone through. Did I join the Khmer Rouge because of the black shirt I was wearing? And how long could I stay? I told them the story of the black shirt, they were relieved, and that I could only stay for two days.

I was surprised to see my older brother at home with my parents. He told me that he had escaped just a short month after we left home. My parents were also glad that he was home, as he was able to fish for the family a protein-rich food source in these times of scarcity. I was relieved to hear this and see him safe with my own eyes. It was because of the friendship between my parents and their group leader that he was still able to stay home safely with them and work in the village with villagers. I had no idea what would happen in the future, but right now everything seemed okay. I wondered what happened to our cows and the wagon. Mom said they were taken away about a week later after I left for labor camp. Not just our cows, but the rest of the village experienced the same.

Moreover, my mother stated that the Khmer Rouge had eliminated temples and monks, and there was no exemption for monks in terms of work. The Khmer Rouge believed that people who became monks were lazy and did not want to work. Therefore, they required every monk to go to work just like the rest of the people.

Dad said mom prayed every day for my safety, and that she kept her head shaved until she knew I was still alive. Dad said that Mom cried all the time because she thought I might be dead since other kids in our village came home from the same labor camp, but she didn't hear any news about me at all.

Then, the parents of the girls that were in the group, came to see me. They brought food to give to me. They heard that I brought Yerm home, they asked many questions about their daughters, and in addition, they requested that I bring their daughters when I come next time. I was at a loss for words and did not know what to say. All I could promise was that I would try. In fact, I did not know if I could come again or not. I then gave the letter that the girls asked me to write to their parents. Some asked me to read for them as well. Parents had tears in their eyes from hearing me read those letters.

After those parents left, my family and I were talking the whole night. My parents told me that after I left, the Khmer Rouge had assigned 10 families to one group and each group had one leader and assistant to the leader; these people were the villagers. She said the leader of our group was a very nice young man about 30 years old. He was married with one baby about 8 months old. Both the husband and wife were very nice and helpful. The leader saw mom getting skinnier and skinnier, he told her to stay to babysit his child instead of going to work in a field that requires strength. Mom said that staying at home to babysit was much easier than cutting down trees in the woods or working on a rice farm. This way she had more time at home to grow vegetables on the side of the house too.

I told my parents how this visit was possible, starting from the story of my blouse and because I would take food back to the work camp for people there. I also told them, I needed to talk to the group leader to ask for whatever he could give to me to take back with me. Mom said that she did not see any problem.

I asked her if I should go to Yeam's house because her parents had invited me over for dinner. Mom said that the villagers had been without rice for a while now because the Khmer Rouge decided to reduce supply, but luckily there were plenty of sweet potatoes that everyone in the village substituted for rice. Mom pointed to the corner where there was a big pile of sweet potatoes. Mom said we had plenty too.

That evening mom cooked a few dishes of food for dinner and for me to take with me when I went back. It felt so good to be home, to eat together as a family, to be able to talk to my parents, brother, and sister, and to be able to sleep in the same home with my family. It was a wonderful feeling.

We went to see the family's group leader the next day. His wife was very nice and offered me some food. Then we went to get Yeam so that we could go together. He took us to meet one of the people in charge of the village. He kindly told us that he would put together what was available at the time for us to take with us.

Yeam and I spent the rest of the day running around different parts of the village, collecting food from different groups. We got two big bags that consisted of varieties of fruits, vegetables, potatoes, banana trunks, and fish. Due to the high tide season, my brother was able to catch lots of fish for the family and me.

When I spent time with my mother that night, she gave me gold necklaces that she was able to hide from the Khmer Rouge. She made a belt from cloth and put a necklace in there. She told me to always wear it on my waist and escape to Thailand if possible, and that the gold would be for me to use for necessities like food and shelter. She told me not to worry about anything or anyone at home and just go find freedom if the opportunity presented itself. Once again, I cried. I told her that I would not go away and never come home, however, she insisted that if given the chance, I must find freedom and leave Cambodia as soon as possible because there was no future here anymore.

Time flew by quickly, and it was time to return. I left the black shirt for my parents as I knew it would be useful to them one day. I said goodbye to my family again, but this time it was not so bad because my parents knew that even though I had to work labor jobs, which no one could avoid, I would be all right. My mom felt more relaxed than before. I was happy to see her feeling that way.

My brothers and a few other villagers helped us get the food to the boat. It was quite a distance to the dock, so my brother arranged for a cow with a wagon to transport our supplies.

I arrived at the dock and found several parents waiting for me. Again, they asked if I could bring their daughter on my next visit if possible, and I told them that I would try. The parents handed me packages of food to take to their daughters. I felt good about having achieved my goal. I was able to see my family and bring some food back with me, so I was able to share it with the group.

On the journey back, a sense of relaxation washed over me. Accomplishing my goal filled me with a great sense of satisfaction. Sitting on the boat, I took a moment to admire the breathtaking scenery that enveloped us as the tranquil water stretched out in all directions, showcasing the beauty of nature.

Finally, we arrived at the dock and carefully unloaded the bags of food. There was no way that we could carry such an amount back to the camp by ourselves. We had to wait for assistance. After about an hour, a man driving a cow wagon happened to pass by. We approached him, asking if he would be willing to give us a ride if he was going in our direction.

A kind man helped load the bags of food onto the wagon, and we were very thankful for it. Yeam and I jumped onto the wagon. Just as we were about to depart, I overheard someone asking for directions to Phnom Sress. The voice sounded just like my older sister. I quickly turned around to look at who was speaking, and to my joy, it was indeed my sister. It was a miracle! I just saw my family here in Phnom Sress, now my sister. Without hesitation, I asked the driver to wait while I ran over to greet her. She was equally surprised and delighted to see me. I asked how she ended up here, and how she was faring.

My sister explained that she had been deeply concerned about our parents ever since we last parted ways. Determined to find them, she sought permission from her village leader to embark on a journey to search for our parents. She was traveling with her father-in-law, who was also looking for his missing relatives. However, our conversation was cut short as the wagon driver called out that it was time to depart. I shared with my sister the incredible news that I had just seen our family. They had been relocated to Phnom Sress, and now my sister expressed her strong desire to see them.

With little time to spare, I quickly provided her with directions on how to reach Phnom Sress and emphasized the need for a boat as the primary mode of transportation. I told her that there was an East side and a West side of Phnom Sress to make sure that she went to the right side, which was the EAST. After conveying these instructions, I embraced her tightly, expressing my heartfelt goodbye. Reluctantly, I jumped back onto the wagon and the man resumed driving. I watched my sister fade into the distance.

The return journey by cow wagon was not only faster but also more pleasant compared to traveling by foot. When we arrived, everyone was still at work. As soon as they caught sight of me, they eagerly approached, bombarding me with numerous inquiries about their families. Being able to bring joy to so many individuals filled me with a sense of fulfillment and satisfaction. It was a wonderful feeling knowing that my actions had made a positive impact on their lives.

A few more weeks passed, and Yeam got very sick. She developed a persistent high fever that lasted for several days. Her condition continued to deteriorate despite our efforts. She could not eat, or sleep and her condition continued to deteriorate. Concerned for her well-being, our group leader made necessary arrangements for her to be taken to the hospital.

The hospital, if it could be called that, was in one of the open buildings used by the Khmer Rouge. It lacked a proper wall, only having a roof to provide minimal shelter. The medical staff consisted of young children

It was a frightening sight to witness children, some of them as young as seven years old or possibly younger, carrying weapons and assuming roles as doctors within the hospital. These children had been brainwashed by the Khmer Rouge regime. Education was not a priority to them as they immediately thrust themselves into a position of authority and responsibility.

The communist Khmer Rouge especially targeted children because they were more susceptible to manipulation and control. By instilling their ideology at a young age, they could mold them into obedient followers. It was a disturbing manifestation of the regime's tactics, exploring the innocence and vulnerability of children for their own purposes.

Seeing such young children tasked with roles beyond their eyes was a stark reminder of the extent of the Khmer Rouge's influence and the extraordinary circumstances we found ourselves in.

The medications provided at the hospital were rudimentary and limited in variety. Most of the remedies consisted of palm sugar and various types of tree bark. The bark would be toasted, ground into powder, mixed with palm sugar, and rolled into small round pills. Regardless of the illness or condition, there seemed to be one kind of medication available without any differentiation.

In the cases where the patient's condition was not likely to improve, their resort was to be given an injection. It was a daunting prospect, as the only substance known to be used for injection was coconut water. The thought of receiving an injection of such a basic solution was scary just to think of.

Even if we weren't ill, some of us found the palm sugar pill appealing simply because of its sweet taste. We would often request a handful of pills from kid doctors, claiming to have a headache or stomachache, just to satisfy our craving for the sweetness of palm sugar.

Although these pills did not serve any real medicinal purpose for us, they provided a temporary indulgence and a small source of comfort amidst the harsh realities of our daily lives. The sweetness of the palm sugar offered a brief respite from the challenges and hardships faced under the Khmer Rouge.

After Yeam's departure to the hospital, a series of illnesses struck our group. One by one, my companions fell ill, leaving only two of us remaining from our village: Thou and myself.

As months went by, my bond with Chan grew stronger. She had shown great enthusiasm and determination in learning the alphabet and vowels, which facilitated her progress in reading and writing. It was a rewarding experience for both of us, witnessing her gradual development of these skills. However, our hopes for continuing our educational journey together were dashed when the Ungaleer decided to relocate her to a different location.

Despite the separation, our connection remained intact. On the day of her departure, she expressed her gratitude for the time we had spent together, learning, and growing. She embraced me tightly and expressed her sincere wish that our paths would cross again in the future. The farewell was bittersweet, but the memory of our shared learning experience would remain with us forever.

Following the departure of my previous group leader, a new leader was assigned to our group. However, this new leader proved to be quite different from the previous one. She lacked friendliness and kindness, making the atmosphere within our group much more challenging. To make matters worse she brought someone along to take over the cooking responsibility, which meant that I was once again assigned to work in the water. Although the circumstances became more difficult, I tried to maintain a positive mindset. I reminded myself of a fortunate encounter I had with the compassionate and friendly group leader.

One afternoon, to our surprise we were granted dismissal from work early. This occurrence had never happened, and it sparked curiosity among all of us. As we gathered, each of us was presented with a vibrant colorful scarf. We could not help but wonder about the reason behind the unexpected gesture.

Soon, we were informed of the purpose of our early release and the scarf gifts. The following day, a government representative would be visiting our worksite, and it was emphasized that we needed to be well-rested and prepared. We were instructed to wear our best clothes for the occasion to ensure that there were no holes or mismatched patches. For those who lacked finer clothes, arrangements would be made to borrow one for them.

Additionally, we were told to put on a cheerful demeanor and enthusiastically wave our hands to greet the visitors. The intention behind this instruction was to create an impression of good treatment and contentment within us. The Khmer Rouge attempted to showcase to the visitor's dignitary, whomever they may be, that the Ungaleer was treating us well.

The next morning, a noticeable change occurred in our routine. We were granted a break from our usual 5 am call, instead we were allowed to sleep in until about 7 am.

Unexpectedly, no visitors arrived. It was a rather quiet and uneventful period. As lunchtime approached, we made our way to the road where we typically had our lunch, and we were surprised to see what we were going to have for lunch. It was plenty of cooked rice and a delicious grilled salty fish. It was a feast unlike any we had experienced in a very long time. I did not remember when the last time was, I had eaten such a savory and delicious fish.

Throughout the day and into the night, the air resonated with the melody of music, as was customary on every job site to inspire and uplift our spirits amidst the toil of our daily tasks. The rhythmic tunes served as a constant backdrop, infusing a sense of rhythm and energy into our laborious routine.

A few hours after lunch, our attention was drawn to the sight of several Jeeps approaching our vicinity. A few people were inside these vehicles, but their identities were concealed by the tinted windows.

They did not halt their progress, but instead drove at a slow pace, allowing us a fleeting glimpse of their presence. From a distance, some of them did not look like the Khmer Rouge. Perhaps there were some other authorities from different parts of the country or different parts of the world, only they knew.

As the Jeeps made their way past our worksite, the occupants signaled their presence with a resounding honk of their horns. In response, the Khmer Rouge guards who monitored our activities waved their hands in acknowledgment. In just a few minutes, the Jeeps passed by. We could only wonder about the significance of those passing vehicles and the purpose of their visit. The true nature of their mission remained shrouded in mystery.

A few days later, we were relocated to a different area where there was a shallow water source, allowing us to resume the construction of levees. Our previous location had proven unsuitable due to the deep water and the strong current. In this new area, the water was about a foot deep, which made our work more manageable. We were able to build miles of levees, each measuring approximately 2 feet wide by 4 feet high.

As time passed, we noticed the change in the behavior of the Khmer Rouge. They seemed to be losing focus, and their credibility started to waver. To stretch the limited food supply, they began adding more water to our meals, which made us feel hungry sooner. The reason behind this decision remained unknown, and we could only speculate about their motives. Nevertheless, their diminishing effectiveness was evident, and we were left uncertain about what lay ahead.

After careful consideration and discussion, some of us reached a unanimous decision; we wanted to go home. The prevailing sense that the Khmer Rouge was losing their grip on control gave us a glimmer of hope and opportunity to escape. However, we understood the risk involved and knew that we had to plan our escape meticulously to ensure our safety. In the end, we were afraid and chose not to proceed with our plan. The daunting and uncertain consequences proved too overwhelming, causing us to ignore our aspiration of escape.

1 4

The Malaria

A few weeks later, our newly assigned leader was unexpectedly reassigned to another location, leaving us without a leader. The unexpected change was not just in our group, many others experienced the same. With no instructions or responsibilities, we seized the opportunity and made a unanimous decision: it was time to go home. A sense of joy and relief washed over us as we eagerly gathered our belongings, preparing for a long-awaited journey back to our loved ones.

We were so happy too soon, as our plans were abruptly disrupted. Moments after we finished packing, a few Khmer

Rouge members on bicycles approached us. They commanded us to pack our belongings once again, informing us that we were to be transferred to another labor camp further away. They assured us that they would lead the way. In their unfamiliarity with us, a daring idea came to mind. As soon as they departed, I resolved to find an opportunity to secretly turn back and make my way home without their knowledge.

I shared my plan with Thou, the girl from the same village, hoping she would join me in going home. However, to my disappointment, she expressed her concern about the risks involved and the possibility of getting caught. She confessed that going home would only help her a little, as she had no close relatives in the village and her living situation with her aunt's family was far from ideal. While I was hesitant about taking on the journey alone, having already made the trip once before gave me a sense of courage. After careful consideration, I made up my mind to proceed alone.

The peak of the elevated tide season had passed, and I was certain that I would find my way back home. I grabbed my backpack and hid in a nearby bush, patiently waiting for the opportunity to make my move. After several hours, the coast was clear as everyone, including Thou, departed from the area.

Emerging from my hiding spot, I was surprised to discover a small group of individuals also emerging from a nearby bush. Though we were strangers to one another, we shared a common goal, to return home. Everyone lived in a different part of town, far away from my destination, however, they were familiar with the route, particularly the path leading through Phnom Sress. This was a stroke of luck for me, as their knowledge and guidance would prove invaluable during our journey together. The one challenge and uneven road now seemed more manageable, as I had grown accustomed to its hardships and my feet had developed a tougher resilience. After a few hours of walking, the sight of a Phnom Sress came into view. It was at this point that we parted ways, with me continuing my path and others continuing toward their respective home.

As I entered the village, a somber silence engulfed the surroundings. It was evident that most of the villagers were away at work, leaving behind only a handful of adults and young children. The scene was disheartening, as I observed several young children aged between 3 and 5, sitting along on the roadside. Their frail bodies were emaciated, their heads and stomachs disproportionately large, and their torn clothing unable to cover them from the elements. It appears there was an abundance of these vulnerable children, perhaps orphaned or left to fend for themselves. Unable to ignore their plight, I followed the sound of voices, leading me to a gathering of concerned villagers engaged in conversation.

As I approached the scene, my attention was drawn to a distressing scene unfolding before me. I witnessed a cow wagon being driven by two male Khmer Rouge members. To my horror, a man with his hands tightly bound by a rope was being mercilessly pulled behind the wagon. His emaciated body bore the scars and injuries inflicted by the merciless grating. Deeply disturbed, I turned to the villagers, seeking an explanation for the horrifying sight. Their murmurs confirmed a disturbing tale, it was rumored that the man had resorted to the unthinkable act of consuming his child. The words echoed in my ears, leaving me stunned and my mouth gaped open with the unimaginable horror that unfolded during those dark times.

I listened in disbelief as the villagers continued their grim account. The village had been plagued by severe food shortage, pushing everyone to the brink of desperation. This man, in his struggle to keep his child alive, had made a harrowing decision. Overwhelmed by sickness and starvation, he resorted to the unthinkable act of slashing his child and using the body part as a food source. The chilling cries and disturbing commotion alerted the neighboring residents, who in shock and horror, reported the incident to the Khmer Rouge authority. A subsequent search of the man's house uncovered the gruesome evidence, with body parts discovered in a cooking pot and the rest hidden beneath the bed. The depth of despair and anguish that could drive someone to such a desperate act was unimaginable, leaving me haunted by the depths of suffering endured during those tumultuous times.

The man was punished for eating his child. How could an individual be so horrible to eat his child, what went through his psyche? Nobody knew. The man was pulled by the cow cart driven by the Khmer Rouge until his death. I was unable to remain to observe any longer, so I raced to my parent's home.

When I arrived, it was very quiet. I went up the steps to search for my folks. My heart began beating, there was no one home and nothing left inside. It was unpredictably vacant. Where did all my family go? My tears fell and I was so terrified. What happened to everyone? I did not want to think of the worst.

I rushed to the family group leader's home, only to find that he had already left. Tragically, he had been killed by the Khmer Rouge due to an illicit affair he had with a female villager. The woman's husband had passed away from sickness, as he couldn't access proper medical treatment, and their baby had also succumbed to malnutrition. Furthermore, this same woman got involved with a family leader, which was strictly forbidden, and they were caught by the Khmer Rouge. As a result, both were executed.

Learning about this heartbreaking incident came from the group leader's wife, who shared these sorrowful events with me. She also revealed that my family had moved to Phum Sroa Moch. The relocation had been requested by our family members already residing there, and it was ultimately approved by the Khmer Rouge about a couple of months ago. At that moment, I didn't have all the intricate details, but the news of my family's well-being brought me immense relief knowing that they were all safe.

Then I started to worry about myself, how could I get there? Was I allowed to relocate as well? I was alone now, and since my family no longer lives here, would the Khmer Rouge allow me to go? So many questions that I needed to have answered. I asked the family group leader's wife what I should do, and if I could go at any point. She said that I needed to have proper permission. She advised me to consult the new village leader. He was a new Khmer Rouge who arrived in the village a few months ago.

Summoning my courage, I decided to meet the new village leader and lay out my circumstances before him. I hoped that he would be understanding and grant me the consent I needed to be reunited with my family in Phum Sroa Moch.

The new village leader was a man in his early fifties with a small figure and hints of gray hair. He stayed in one of the prominent houses in the village. It had been a while since I had encountered an individual Khmer Rouge member at this age. Surprisingly, he emanated a sense of kindness and compassion. He insisted that I address him by his name, Da Jant. The prefix "Da" denoted a respectful term akin to "grandpa," adding a touch of familiarity and warmth to our interaction. Despite the hardship and turmoil that surrounded us, Da Jant stood out as a benevolent figure, offering a glimmer of hope in an otherwise challenging environment. Da Jant graciously offered me food and reassured me that there was no need to worry.

As we sat on the front porch having our meal, he expressed the intention to assist me in making arrangements to relocate to Phum Sroa Moch. During a conversation that lasted for a few hours, I began to sense a deep regret within him for his involvement with the Khmer Rouge. Da Jant disclosed that before joining the movement, he had been employed by a businessman. His words carried a tone of remorse and he told me to be patient while he sought to discuss my situation with the higher authority. I felt a mix of gratitude and disappointment as Da Jant returned with the unfortunate news. Despite his efforts, the higher authority above him had deemed it impossible for me to relocate. The reason cited was the lack of manpower in the village, and I was instructed to continue until further notice. Overwhelmed by sadness and fear, I struggled to find words to express my emotions for ultimately having no choice but to accept the situation for the time being. I was assigned to a new group of recently arrived individuals from different parts of the country who had not yet been sent to distant labor camps.

Along with many other young people, I stayed in one of the shelters, which only had a roof. It was the season of planting rice crops, and we worked in the shallow water. Everyone was friends when we worked together. During those days, I made a good friend with one of the girls named Thornt. She was one year younger than me. We became close friends. We shared food and spent much time together at work and off work. As time went by, many people got Malarious. I was not sure if this disease was contagious or not. Every other week, someone would get sick.

Then it was my turn to get malaria. This disease made me feel extremely cold on the inside of my body. The chill was so strong in my bones that my whole body was shaking. After the episode was over, I was extremely hot and then the heat went away. Then I felt completely normal and very hungry, but food was limited.

In the beginning, the Khmer Rouge did not believe that we had malaria or that we were very sick. They said we were faking. After all, we didn't want to work because, by the time the episode of malaria was over, we would become normal and hungry. If we had proper food, we would recover sooner. Then, one or more of the Khmer Rouge. had the same sickness, and then they believed that we were being truthful.

I was unable to take care of myself when malaria symptoms attacked. Each time when that happened, people around me tried to help by putting extra layers of blankets over me and lying over me to help me not to shake too much. It helped a little to prevent me from shaking too much, but it didn't help the chills because it was from inside my body not from the weather. My body was hurting all over from the strength that was used to fight the disease. Thornt always helped me whenever she could by getting food, water, and other things, but her help was limited. I was very sick and weak. Some people died from this disease.

The first day I had malaria symptoms was at about 11 am, the total episode lasted several hours. Every day it would start again about ten minutes later, so I knew in advance when malaria would hit. I learned that my brother was still here, working and staying in boys' labor camps not too far from me. After he found out that I was sick, he would stop by briefly to check on me and drop off some cooked fish. He realized that good nutrition would help to give me some strength. Even so, I was still very weak. It took so much of my energy to fight the disease. Regardless, we were brother and sister, but our meetings were limited. So far it had been a few weeks since I had been sick.

The Khmer Rouge never cared about us, they never came by to see how we were doing. The only time they checked on us was to make sure we were off to work. One day my brother showed up at my shelter and told me that he would take me home to our parents. I was so weak that I didn't ask him more, I just wanted to go home. Due to the high tide season, water was everywhere. Boats were the only way to travel. I couldn't walk on my own, so he helped carry me to the boat and rowed to Phum Sroa Moch. My parents were relieved when I got home and so was I. I was so happy to see them and to be home.

I learned that my brother too was not permitted to relocate with my parents. He worked for the village of Phnom Sress, and his shelter was not too far from mine. He was able to find a boat and row to see my parents most of the time at night and told my parents that I had malaria. Mom was worried that I might die if no one helped take care of me. She asked permission from the family leader in Phum Sroa Moch to go to the village of Phnom Sress to ask if she could bring me home.

Despite the initial resistance from the group leader, my mother was determined to bring me back home and take care of me. She made the courageous decision to go once again, this time carrying the only valuable thing that she had left which was her gold ring as a bargaining chip. Although wearing jewelry was strictly prohibited by the Khmer Rouge, the allure of the gold ring was irresistible in such desperate circumstances. Surprisingly, permission was granted, and my mother embarked on a boat to Phnom Sress to meet Da Jant. This time, with his assistance, arrangements were made for both me and my brother to return home. It was my brother who came to fetch me, making the long-awaited reunion with my family.

I was wondering about our family relocating. Mom told me that the village of Phnom Sress was in a dangerous situation because they distributed rice to the villagers less and less as days went by. Many people were struggling to survive. Mom was able to use my black shirt that I left for them to exchange for some rice from a villager. A few of the villagers that were originally from Phnom Sress had more food supply than others. My parents knew that they needed to do something to get out of the situation. Mom's job was to look for vegetables for the villagers, including water spinach that was grown by the river. Therefore, the group leader assigned a boat for her to gather water spinach. In those days, after she got a full boat of vegetables, she was able to find a way to communicate with a family that was in Phum Sroa Moch.

With their friendship and the help from Da Jant, our family was able to move to Phum Sroa Moch.

I felt much better under the care of my parents. A few weeks later, I was back to normal. The family group leader advised us that I must leave for work since I was better. He confirmed that I could stay in the group village, but I had to move to the camp as young people were not allowed to stay home.

At that time, some young people had returned home from labor camps, while there were also new arrivals in the village. The village leader preferred to keep as many workers as possible to help with various tasks of work. Therefore, if the Khmer Rouge did not come to the village to collect young people, the village's leader would prefer to keep us in the village. It meant more work could be done for the village. Like many others, I was assigned to live in the village's camp, which was not too far from the village. I gave my new scarf to my parents before I departed, as I knew it would be useful for them one day.

Fortunately, my older brother was able to build me a decent individual shelter that could shelter me from rain.

We were all assigned to different kinds of jobs based on what needed to be done at that time such as clearing weeds in the field, building mini levees, or replaning rice crops. This was the first time working with the villagers since I had relocated from Phnom Sress. It was still in the high flooding season; we needed boats to travel from place to place. Working in the village's camp was much easier than labor camp. We typically started work at about 7 am and worked until noon, which was an hour lunch break. We worked until 6-9 pm depending on the nature of the job.

One morning as I was just about to leave for work, I was surprised to see one of my 5-year-old younger sisters. She seemed lost and out of place, so I asked her what she was doing here. I reminded her that she was supposed to be at home with our parents. She said that a new kid leader had been assigned by the Khmer Rouge and they were tasked with taking all children from Phum Sroa Moch to a child labor camp.

About twenty children were already collected from the village and were instructed to stay in a group while the leader made plans for them. My sister wandered off and hoped to find me because she didn't want to go to the labor camp. I was worried and I pulled her into my shelter telling her not to come out until I returned from work. And I told her that she MUST follow my directions.

As I walked to work, my mind was racing with worries for my sister and other children. I couldn't imagine them being taken away to a labor camp. At their ages, what kind of work did they expect these children to do? I tried to focus on my work in the rice field, but my thoughts kept going back to the children.

It was around 9 am while working with a new female Khmer Rouge member who was not friendly. We were replanting rice crops about 500 feet away from a new levee that had recently been built. As I was working, I heard my 5-year-old sister calling out to me for help. At first, I thought I must be imagining things, but when I turned to look, I saw her from a distance with her arms tied behind her back. My heart sank and said, "That is my sister." At that moment, I did not think about anything and accepted helping her. I dropped everything I was doing and ran towards her as fast as I could. The female Khmer Rouge member shouted for me to return to work, but I ignored her comment and continued running toward my sister. When I reached her, I saw that her arms were tied very tightly behind her back. She was frightened, hurt, and crying. She told me that she had been hungry and had gone out to look for something to eat when the children's leader saw her and tied her up.

The female Khmer Rouge continued to call out, "Come back now or I put you and your sister in the same hole," and then she fired a gunshot into the air. I knew that I must return, or I might get killed. I was unable to untie her completely, but I was able to lose the tightness in her arm. I told her that I must return to work and told her to go where the camp was to avoid getting hurt and I would figure things out later. I ran back to work quickly and apologized to the Khmer Rouge. She warned me not to let that happen again.

As I continued to work, I couldn't focus on anything but the safety of my younger sister. I was worried about her being sent to the child labor camp. Would they punish her and what kind of work she would be forced to do? I knew that the only thing I could do was to pray for her safety and hope that she would be able to survive whatever hardship she was going to face. The thought of not being able to protect my sister haunted me, but I had to be strong for her.

During our lunch break, I told my fellow workers about the situation with the children. They were all just as worried as I was. We knew that we had to do something to help them. But what could we do? We were just powerless workers.

After finishing work, I went back to my shed and was startled to see my sister roasting potatoes on the campfire near my shed, the place I used for cooking. I became anxious and worried about her safety. I quickly grabbed her hand and took her inside the shed. I asked her how she had managed to get here, and she told me that she didn't want to go to the child labor camp and had untied herself after I had loosened the ropes on her arms. She then searched for my shed and found her way here. Despite feeling relieved that she was safe, I was also frightened and angry at her for putting herself in danger.

I told her to stay inside and not to leave the shed at all while I went to search for my younger brother. He was around 13 years old at that time and had been assigned by the new Khmer Rouge to transport food and perform other tasks. As a result, he had access to the boat or a cow wagon and could easily take our sister back home to our parents. After searching for about an hour, I was able to find him and arranged for him to take our sister home. A few hours later, my brother returned, and I was relieved to learn that my sister was safely back home with our parents.

One of the tasks required us to walk past Phnom Sress to reach our work site. After a few days of walking this route, I decided to make a quick stop to visit Da Jant, informing my coworkers to continue to the job site, and that I would catch up. I intended to briefly stop by and express my gratitude in person for his assistance in reuniting me and my brother with our parents. Upon arriving at Da Jant's residence, I discovered he was nowhere to be found. Inquiring about it from one of the villagers, I learned that he had been seen escorted by two male Khmer Rouge soldiers about a week ago. It appeared that he was facing some sort of trouble. Even since that day, Da Jant had not been spotted. Concern for his safety overwhelmed me, and I nearly felt like I was about to faint.

---

1 5

Working in The Contaminated Water

A few more days passed, and I found out that there was a water stream that was close to the job site which I could swim across to **Phum Sroa Moch** where my parents lived in about 15 minutes. Then I would walk another 15 minutes through the cemetery to get home. This way I could spend more time at home. So, every other day, I would go straight to see my parents after work by swimming across the stream with a few of my coworkers rather than returning to the camp. Some people warned me that there may be alligators or snakes in the stream that would harm me. I was concerned, but my desire to go home was much stronger than my fear. If I showed up at work on time it would not be a problem. I would stay overnight sometimes. In that case, I had to get up early and swim back to the job site where I would arrive at about the same time as other people. I knew that early morning swimming was cold, but after all, I never got this kind of chance to spend time with my parents, so I would take the opportunity whenever I could. A couple of times when I swam across the stream, I encountered a snake. In those cases, I just swam away fast to get away from it. I believed it was a water snake and might be no harm to me if I did not disturb it; just my thoughts.

Then one day, a few of the Khmer Rouge came to the village and collected young people again, as was their routine. They would check out the village every so often to make sure that no young people stayed there since we belonged at the labor camp. They visited the rice field and when they saw us, they notified the village leader that they were not allowed to keep young people in the village. We had to gather our belongings and go with them.

My few weeks of enjoying working close by with my family came to an end. I along with a few others had to leave our families again. After about half a day of walking, we arrived at a new job site. They told us to leave our belongings aside and follow them. They took us to another job site involving working inside the water to pull weeds and prepare the soil for the next rice crop. It was deep inside the field far from the road and we had to walk about thirty minutes each way to work. There were several shelters alongside the road and there was just the roof and one side of the wall. There were about fifty of us there.

Our legs were sore and very red after only a few days of work. It stung terribly and had a burning sensation before it began to blister, then blisters popped and tore off the skin and it was wet and sticky. Even walking was challenging for us. It resembled a snake shedding its skin. Our skin erupted because of the water's quality, which was either overly rich in soil or tainted with something. Some of the Khmer Rouge experienced the same issue. When that happened, it was much simpler for us to take a few days off.

The next few weeks, we took turns staying out of the water, so that our skin had time to grow back. If we stayed off the water for a few days, our skin would dry and peel off and the new skin would begin to regenerate. We occasionally made remarks regarding the length of time it would take for our scars to fade or whether they would ever heal normally. Would we live long enough to tell these stories to our children and grandchildren?

We spent a couple of months at this location but never got to finish all the jobs assigned to us. One day the two Khmer Rouge that were watching over us had disappeared;

we had no idea where they went. Then a few hours later, two other different Khmer Rouge showed up to replace them. They were different from the previous. We were confused. It looked like there were two different groups of Khmer Rouge. We did not know what was going on. They transferred us to another job site. We were relieved that we didn't need to work inside the tainted water.

When we arrived at the new job site, there were hundreds of people working on the road to build another levee. Our tasks were to dig a hole that was 7 feet long, 4 feet wide, and 2 feet deep for each person per day, and then transport the dirt to another location by yoke, which could be anywhere from 20 to 50 feet away. At first, it was not too difficult, but as days went by, the piles of dirt accumulated like small mountains connected to one another, and we had to pour new dirt onto the high part. If we could not finish our assigned tasks, we would not be allowed to have dinner and we would have to stay until it was completed. I worked as fast as I could along with some other people. By about 2 pm, I had finished my assignment for the day along with a few others, and we had the rest of the day off.

A few days later, the Khmer Rouge added more work for us because we finished our tasks too quickly. After that, we worked at a normal pace and didn't want to rush to get it done early because we knew that they would just give us even more work. Some of us could have completed the additional work early too, but we chose not to, to avoid getting more work.

After a few days, I saw a new group of people arriving at the location. These were the people that had been evacuated from their hometown far away from here just like many of us worked here.

I learned that some of them were evacuated from their town at times when they were not home. Therefore, they had no idea where the rest of their families were. I could imagine one of the children might be with friends or at the market, anywhere else but home. I could relate to that as I was lucky to return to my hometown in Mongkol Borey to my family just one night when we were evacuated.

Additionally, this was their initial assignment to the labor camp. These new groups of people lacked sufficient food. They appeared tired and thin. They seemed to struggle with the labor work and It was clear that they were not accustomed to this kind of work and lifestyle. No one had anticipated such a treatment from the new government, which claimed to be rescuing the nation and its people. I noticed that some of them were carrying cans filled with worms, which was their food. It was a situation I sympathized with, as I knew the feeling of being extremely hungry and needing to eat whatever was available to survive. I was fortunate enough, however, not to have to eat worms to survive, not yet anyway, and I hope I won't have to.

Some of the new groups of individuals were not able to finish the daily assignment. I witnessed them having to work very late; the Khmer Rouge made them work until dark. As days went by, more and more loads were added up to those who could not finish their daily work. I felt so bad to see that some of them were struggling. What would happen to them as the days went by? It filled me with dread just thinking about it.

1 6

Escaping from A Labor Camp to See My Dying Little Sister

A few more months passed. One day, I was feeling uneasy and had this urge to go home. I tried to ignore it because I knew that it was impossible, and I didn't want to take any risk. A couple of days later, I still felt the same way, it did not matter how much I neglected it. I didn't know why I had this urgent feeling, I just wanted to go home. But what was I supposed to do? I decided to talk to a few of my close co-workers. The idea of going home made them interested and they considered it. I felt restless these past few days, so I decided to make my own decision.

The next day during work, I had to convince three people from the same village to go with me just in case I could not find my way home because I knew that I was not good at finding my direction. I told them that we needed to go tonight because I could not wait any longer, and we planned to escape at midnight while everyone was asleep. In the beginning, there were four of us, then one changed their mind. She told us to just go, and she would find a reason to cover up if the Khmer Rouge ever found out we were missing.

The time had come, it was dark and quiet, and everyone was asleep. We slept in a row one after another. I sat up and tapped one person next to me and she tapped the other. We woke up slowly and walked quietly and realized that it was just me and another girl named Sother. The other girl was too afraid and decided not to go, but it did not stop us.

We walked fast but quietly so we would not make any noise. Just about 5 minutes or so later, we saw a light pointing in our direction. It was dark, we could not tell what that was and we were frightened. The light was approaching so fast that we could not hide. It was a Khmer Rouge soldier riding a bicycle toward us. He stopped and yielded "Friend, where are you going?" I had to respond fast before he pulled his gun on us. I told him that we were walking to the bathroom. That was how we needed to do our things, which involved walking further into the woods. He told us to hurry and go back to the camp and then he continued with his bike.

We almost gave up. We waited for a while for the bike to go far enough, then we continued to walk for a few more hours, and suddenly I felt like I was stepping into a pothole filled with water. I stood there and looked at it carefully, I saw it was not a pothole, it was a lake or a big pond or something, I could not tell. It was the edge that I stepped in. The sky was dark; we could not see well enough to tell what it was. What were we going to do? As we moved another step, it got deeper. Now we realized that this was not a small pond. Whatever it was, we had to move on. Luckily both of us could swim. So, we continued to swim slowly. It took us about 30 minutes to swim to the other side, and we were all soaking wet.

A few more hours later, the sun started to rise. We walked past a few villages and some village leaders were friendly. They greeted us when we passed by their village and gave us food if we asked for it. By the time we arrived at Phum Sroa Moch, it was late morning. Sother and I decided we would meet later, and she went to her parent's house, while I went to see my parents.

As I stepped inside, I saw my parents, brothers, and sister were all sitting there quietly and looking depressed. They were surprised to see me arrive unexpectedly. Then my heart dropped as I noticed my four-year-old little sister lying down on the floor, extremely thin. All I could see was her large head, big eyes, and bony body covered with skin, just like a human skeleton. I approached her and picked her up into my arms, tears streaming down my face. My little sister stared at me with her wide eyes open without blinking. She had no strength to talk. I was certain if she could speak, she would ask me "Why did it take you so long? I have been waiting for you." Shortly after, she was struggling for the last breath of her life. She was dying in my arms; I was crying uncontrollably.

I asked Mom what happened to my little sister. She told me that my little sister was very brave and strong. Every day she went with one of the neighbor kids around her age to look for dry wood for mom to use for cooking and always came back with lots. She carried that wood on top of her head. Then one day, a neighbor told mom that her kid told her, when my little sister went to poop, she saw a lot of blood. By that time Mom knew her infection was severe, and Mom had tried every possible way to cure her, but it was impossible without real medication. Mom told me that she had a couple of tablets of antibiotics left that she kept and that one day it would be useful. Then later, someone she knew was very sick, so she decided to give those tablets of antibiotics to the person. Now that her child was sick, she had nothing. It was a couple of tablets of antibiotics; would it heal her infection? If Mom still had that, she believed that somehow it would help a little and that would give her time to find a cure.

Mom said she did not think my little sister could hold on that long. It was hard for my parents to see her like that and feel hopeless that nothing they could do. They knew that it was just a matter of time, so Mom dressed her up in her favorite clothes that mom was able to buy and hide before the Khmer Rouge arrived. She also put gold earrings on for her as well. Mom said that was all she was able to give to her. My mom was a very strong woman.

A couple of hours later, my parents told my brother to wrap her around with floor mats. That was the best they had for that time, to wrap her and take her to be buried. Mom told him to find a spot of high ground to avoid water when it was flood season. I was unable to stop crying and gave my little sister her last hug.

Then, Sother came back. She said we had to go back now before they found out. I cried; I missed my little sister too much to just leave, but I had no other choice, I did not want my family to get into trouble. I said goodbye to them, and Mom packed some food that was available for me to take along. It was very hard for me on the way back to the labor camp. I cried on and off along the way and Sother tried to comfort me and ended up crying too.

It was much easier and faster for us to go back because it was still light outside. By the time we arrived at the camp, it was dark. We snuck inside the camp without anyone noticing us. One of the girls that changed her mind told us that no one knew that we were missing, we were glad to hear that. She also said that there were more new people coming today.

It was dinner time; everyone got their plate to get food. Right as we were about to eat, we heard a loud microphone announcement for an emergency meeting, and dinner was put on hold. The announcement was they knew people were escaping and had been captured. Sother and I looked at each other in alarm, were they talking about us? This question was starting to terrify us.

As we arrived at the meeting, we sat in the group and tried to blend in with many others. I could see five male Khmer Rouge standing in the front and one of them sitting on a tall chair. Two boys who were the same age as me were being held by the Khmer Rouge. The one sitting on a chair started to lecture us about how they would improve the country. They needed us to work hard be honest, and not try to run away from responsibility. We would be punished if they caught us.

After he informed us of his objective, he pointed to the two boys. Those boys were lost while trying to run away from camp and were captured, they looked frightened. Then one of the Khmer Rouge that held the boy, used his gun to hit the boy's head very hard. His head started to bleed, and he fell to the ground. The other boy witnessed the hit, got agitated, and tried to break through and run. He ran just about 25 feet or so before the Khmer Rouge pulled the trigger and shot him from behind. The boy fell when he was shot. The Khmer Rouge walked toward him and shot him a few more times. The boy died on the spot. He returned and shot the other boy and he too died. At the meeting, everyone was very scared, including me. The same thing would happen to me if I was captured. Everyone was silent. He then continued, saying there was no need to keep useless people around. It was just a waste of their food. They would rather keep one cow than ten humans. Cows did not complain like humans.

At that moment, I was so frightened for my life. The fate of the two boys served as a haunting warning. If Sother and I were captured, death awaited us. Yet, an inexplicable urgency to return home overwhelmed me. It was as if my little sister's voice called out to me, urging me to find my way back to her. Taking a chance, I decided to heed that inner call and made the perilous journey home. And I will forever be grateful that I did. It was the last time I saw my dear little sister. A fleeting moment of happiness amidst the turmoil. I could not help but feel that somehow, she was watching over us, protecting us from the danger that lurked at every turn. I was grateful that I took the chance to go home, as it allowed me to see her for the very last time. The memory of that precious encounter remains etched in my heart. Her presence had given me strength, and I cherished every moment we had together. It was a brief respite from the cruel reality of the Khmer Rouge regime, and for that, I will forever hold her close in my thoughts and prayers.

From that day on, I always carried that memory of her with me. She was happy to see me, and I was grateful to be there for her.

The next morning as we made our way to work, a chilling sight greeted us: hands protruding from the ground on the path we walked. Two young boys' bodies lay there, a grim and horrifying display intended to serve as a warning to anyone who dared to contemplate escape. The Khmer Rouge wanted to instill terror in us, to remind us that attempting to flee would lead to the same gruesome fate.

Since then, the walk to our daily labor became a race against those haunting images. We ran as fast as our feet could carry us, eager to pass by the harrowing spot without lingering to look upon the twisted display. The memory of the boys and the warning they represented became a heavy burden on our hearts, fueling our determination to survive this brutal regime.

One evening, one of the new girls I was sleeping next to seemed stressed out. She looked a bit younger than me. I asked if she was alright. She told me that she did not want to be a part of what we were doing and that she did not like it. Every day, she complained about never having enough sleep and food to eat and she was very exhausted. When I heard her say that I started to worry. I tried to convince her that even though we didn't want to, we had our job to do. It was critical to survive. She began to weep. I knew how she felt, but we couldn't do anything.

Several days passed without her going to work. This was noticed by one of the Khmer Rouge, and she began investigating our shelter to determine who was absent from work and why. The same Khmer Rouge woke her up a few more days later in the middle of the night. She said that Ungaleer wanted to talk to her, I heard. The girl never returned. I witnessed a 15-year-old boy digging a hole for a few days without letting him rest. Later, the Khmer Rouge wouldn't let him eat until he finished, but he never did.

The worst was when the boy was kicked in the head by the Khmer Rouge and was covered with dirt while he was still alive. Yes, they buried him alive. They held another meeting and informed us that we would dig our own graves if we didn't want to work.

As days went by, The Khmer Rouge wanted us to work faster each day. As a result, we had to return to work after dinner. Working from 5 a.m. until 6 p.m. with only half an hour for lunch was not enough for them. Now they added evening hours which was after supper until whatever point they wanted us to stop. They created a lively environment by having electricity and music to encourage us.

Due to everyone's daytime exhaustion from work, it did not work out. Additionally, many individuals, I included, developed eye problems that we called "chicken blind." It was like a chicken that can't see in the dark after sunset. I had never experienced anything like this before. After the sunset, I had a hard time seeing things or seeing things blurry. I was scared, I thought I went blind. Later, I learned that poor nutrition was to blame for this disease. At first, they thought we were unmotivated and lazy. Afterward, they understood that it was a significant issue. The night shift was eliminated because so many people had the "chicken blind" condition.

So far, the only holiday that we were allowed to take a day off from work was New Year's Day. There were a few things that happened on that day.

We were able to eat pork, which was given about one kilogram for a group of 30 people. Therefore, we had to cut meat into small pieces and cook it with more water, and we added any vegetables that we could find on that day. Then, we each shared a soup spoon of it, and if there was any leftover after one round, we continued the second or third round.

We would have a dessert. It was cooked rice with lots of water and added palm sugar for a light sweet. Each person would have about an eight-ounce size bowl.

Then, each group would have a bottle of about 16 ounces of orange soda. We would share by the spoonful, and if any were left over, we would go for the second or third round.

And for those guys who wished to get married, he would inform the male Khmer Rouge leader. The male leader would then ask the female Khmer Rouge leader to ask whomever he wanted to marry (these inquiries took place a few weeks or more before the new year.) Then one leader of the Khmer Rouge would simultaneously perform a marriage ceremony for all parties involved if she agreed. It could occur for twenty couples or more annually in different parts of the camp.

Additionally, the Khmer Rouge would give everyone a brand-new scarf as a wedding present. They were then able to return to the village where they had come from because married people would stay and work in the village. That implied they didn't have to work in labor camps far away from home like youthful single individuals. As a result, most people get married without real love or real feelings. They did that to avoid working in the labor camp.

New Year's Day was the day that we had time to get rid of most of our head lice. Each of us had head lice, and there were a lot of them, because we slept next to each other for a long time, and we didn't have shampoo. Not many of us had a comb, therefore we took turns to use the comb. We would comb our hair down using one of the light-colored clothes we had. we would see head lice drop just like black sesame seeds. The comb we had shared was just a regular comb too.

Another week later, we were assigned to a different location to build a roadway. We were at the new location only for a few weeks when someone got sick and died. Then another person got cut while at work, that cut got infected and the infection got worse and about a week later, that person died. Within just about a couple of months, 3 people died from similar incidents, it was weird.

Then I accidentally cut a small piece of skin off my second toe while removing the soil. It was a very tiny cut, the size of the tip of a toothpick. But a few days later, the small cut turned into a larger hole that hurt. I patched it with clear clay, wrapped it with a leaf, and tied it down to keep anything else from getting into the hole because we did not have any medication or bandage. Then one more person got hurt and got infected. The same as the previous person, she died as well. I started to feel very afraid that the cut I had might get worse and eventually kill me. It hurt so badly at night as the weather was cooler, and I felt like something was digging into my wound.

The incident was so weird that it got the Khmer Rouge's attention. We started to believe that it must be a curse at this location and that it was not to be disturbed. We were there for a few months and five people died. We strongly believed that it was a curse, and we must move out as soon as possible before more people die. We held a meeting among ourselves to urge the Khmer Rouge to move out. Due to a weird situation, the Khmer Rouge decided to abandon the project and we moved to different locations.

1 7

Top Selected Group of 100 People for A Frontline Team

One afternoon, a month later, two Khmer Rouge members arrived at the job site. The workers were given instructions to leave work immediately if we heard our names called, as we were being reassigned to a new location. Slowly, one name at a time was called out, and the workers had to start packing up their belongings. My name was also called, along with two other people from the same village. I was feeling relieved to have someone from the same village as I was still worried about the possibility of returning home alone.

They told us that we were the top chosen gathering of 100 individuals to turn into a bleeding edge group, they would move us when and where required with short notice. They knew who to choose because they had been observing us for a few weeks. They gave us each a bowl of cooked rice that we wouldn't normally get. Each of us was also given a brand new black uniform, a new colorful scarf, and a pair of black rubber sandals. They were nice shoes, and after months of working and walking barefoot, I was glad to have them. These materials were typically only available to the Khmer Rouge. They wanted us to feel like we were one of them by giving us these uniforms. We were taken to a new location by a truck an hour later.

This camp was unlike any other, the shed looked decent. They divided us into ten groups, each with a single Khmer Rouge leader. They told us that we had to show the government that we were the dominant force for Ungaleer. Even though our shelter only had a roof and a wall on one side, it was much better than the months we had moving from place to place without shelter.

We were informed that we were about to undertake the construction of a massive levee. This was going to be a significant scale, towering approximately 25 feet high and stretching 10 feet wide. As for the length, it was intended to extend as far as it could. This levee would preserve so much water that we would be able to cultivate rice in the scorching summer months and transfer the water to the rice field.

They assured us that we were all equal and that no one was superior to anyone throughout our time working there. I acknowledge that we were treated better, but we were not even close to equal. Our shelter only had one side, whereas theirs had four walls. Even though they provided us with a bowl of rice each meal, their food was always better than ours.

Out of the 100 of us, one girl named Gayle had a lot in common with me. Individuals felt that we were sisters or cousins. We were not, however, related in any way, and we eventually became close friends. At some point, she brought me good food. I noticed that the Khmer Rouge had this food in their shelter, so I asked her where it came from. Gyle advised me to eat without asking and not be concerned. I initially accepted and thanked her for providing me with delicious food. Every so often, she would give me different kinds of food.

We were awakened one late night by the Khmer Rouge and ordered to stay in line with our group of ten. With some light from the crescent moon, I could tell they were searching for someone, but I had no idea for whom and for what reason. Once they got to my group, one of the female Khmer Rouge looked at us one by one, then she pointed to me "It was her!"

and pulled me out of the line. What was going on? I was clueless. She drugged me in front of one other female Khmer Rouge and said, "I saw, that was her." We were called out to the field in a hurry. I was still half asleep struggling to get up and wondering what was happening. I panicked and replied, "I have no idea what you are talking about, I was asleep when you called out for a meeting." One of the other Khmer Rouge came and stared at me for a good number of minutes. Then she said, "It was not her." I was feeling relief from hearing that. A couple of hours later, I learned that they were looking for Gyle. Gyle snuck into the Khmer Rouge shelter and took their food. Then, I realized how Gyle got all the delicious food, so I kept quiet. Finally, the meeting was over, and Gyle could not be found. I was worried for her and wondering where she was. My mind once again was full of imagination. The only thing that I could do was pray and hope that she would be safe. After that day, I never saw or heard from her again.

A few weeks later, one of the Khmer Rouge appeared at the construction site. She selected ten people to go to different parts of the project. I was one of those ten, nothing else was known about it. We packed our belongings and waited for a truck to pick us up.

1 8

Taking Care of Cotton Plants in The Mountain

The anticipated truck arrived, but it was not what we had imagined. Instead, it resembled a colossal tractor with an extended bed for us to sit on. It took a few hours to get there, and the ride was rough. We arrived at a small village nestled near the foot of the mountain and were greeted by the village's leader. He told us that we were his responsibility and that he would provide us with food and shelter. There was no housing available for us to stay at the moment, so he took us to one of the barns that stored dried corn.

As the barn door swung open, I peered to look inside and saw half of the space filled with corn on the cob. The village's leader explained that this humble barn would serve as a temporary shelter. He promised more suitable accommodation in due time. We didn't mind at all, especially accompanied by an abundance of food, a luxury beyond imagination. During our stay, he informed us that rice was in short supply. Nonetheless, he ensured a small ratio of rice alongside portions of corn. This disparity in food offerings hardly concerned us, as we found ourselves surrounded by piles of provisions each night. We relaxed for the rest of the day.

The following morning, two female Khmer Rouge members escorted us to a cotton farm located in the mountains.

Along the way, we passed by many kinds of fruit farms such as jackfruit, banana, orange, mango, and many others. It was a couple hours of walking distance before we arrived at the cotton farm and there were miles and miles of cotton plants. Our task was to inspect the plants and remove any worms or insects that we found. We would also be responsible for spraying the plants with pesticides. This job was relatively easy compared to the previous assignments. We were taken to a station near the farm where we picked up the hand pump and chemicals to mix for spraying.

The Khmer Rouge gave us a task and introduced us to the location before departing. It was an amazing experience to be in charge of our own work. On the first day, we only worked for a few hours. We took a stroll around the mountain farms' landscape. It was still too early for those fruit trees to produce fruits, but we enjoyed viewing different kinds of flowers from those trees. On the way home from work, the journey was much faster because we were going downhill. It took us half of the time that it took us to go up.

We weren't supposed to consume the corn stored in the barn, but only ten of us would know if we did. Since cooking dry corn took a long time and we didn't have a lot of time, we opted to make popcorn instead. However, the popping of the kernel was quite loud, and we risked attracting unwanted attention. To avoid this, a few of us took turns to keep looking for anyone who might be passing by while the rest made popcorn.

A week later, the village's leader took us to our new accommodation, it was a vacant wooden home. Before leaving the barn, we took as much corn as we could carry. We suspected that the village's leader knew about our actions, but he chose to turn a blind eye. However, we could no longer eat as much as we wanted at this point. To bring it with us to work the following day, we would make popcorn almost every evening. We wrapped the popcorn in the corner of our scarf making it convenient for us to eat when we were hungry. As we settled in, we introduced ourselves became close friends, and talked about our lives and backgrounds.

Later, I learned that one of the girls, Samoan, had relatives living in Phum Makast, which was a couple hour's walk from our location. I thought it would be a great opportunity to try to find my older sister who lived in the same area, now that we were our own boss and had more freedom. I talked to Samoan about the idea of going to see our relatives, and she agreed to accompany me to find my sister while she looked for her own family. However, she did not know where her relatives' house was located. I brought up the idea with the rest of the group, and they did not mind if we went. I told them that I wasn't sure if I would be able to find our relatives, but if we did, we would like to spend one night with them.

The following morning, while the rest of our group went to work, Samoan and I set out to find our relatives. After a couple of hours of walking, we arrived at Phum Makast and started asking the locals if they knew where our relatives lived. To our amazement, the first person we asked turned out to be Samoan's aunt. She led us to her house and offered us lunch. We gladly accepted her hospitality and sat down to a special curry she had prepared.

Despite our initial shock at learning that we had just eaten dog meat, we both felt grateful for the delicious meal. It had been a while since we had tasted anything like that. I thanked Samoan's aunt for her hospitality and asked if she knew the whereabouts of my sister Eang. She replied affirmatively that she knew my sister well and gave me directions to her house. Samoan stayed with her aunt, and I went on my way to my sister's home.

It took me about 15 minutes to reach her house. I was overjoyed to see her. She was doing chores in front of her house when I arrived and when she heard my voice, she turned around and was surprised to see me. She asked me how I found her and why I had traveled so far to see her. I went inside with her, and she introduced me to her in-laws who were also thrilled to see me.

We hugged and exchanged pleasantries, catching up on all that had happened since we last saw each other while I was transporting food from Phnom Sress to the labor camp. We spent the whole evening talking about our experiences, and I updated her on my current situation and our family. It was wonderful to be able to connect with my sister after so long. My sister had prepared extra food for me since she knew that many young people travel without enough food. I also got to see my two-year-old nephew and brother-in-law. My sister and I talked all night until we both fell asleep.

The next morning, I said goodbye and thanked my sister, brother-in-law, and her parents-in-law. I was feeling content and grateful for the opportunity to see my sister.

After visiting my sister, I headed to Samoan's aunt house. She kindly gave Samoan and me some food to take back with us, which made us very happy. Our journey had been successful, and we made it back just before the rest of our group arrived from work. We took a moment to relax and shared stories about our day, and when our group saw us, they were eager to know if we had brought back any food. To their delight, we brought back some food to share with everyone, and we had a wonderful dinner that evening.

A couple of weeks later, our food supply dwindled, and we were running low. Even though the cotton plants had not yet produced cotton, they began to bear a lot of young cotton fruits. It took time, however, for them to develop, much like many other plants. As we searched for insects on the cotton plants, we picked and ate the young cotton fruits because we learned that they were edible and quite delicious. Its taste was crunchy and lightly sweet, and we could only eat a few at a time, being careful not to strip all the fruits from their plants. Most of the time, we survived on corn from the barn since we did not have rice.

Every day after work, we would scavenge for food. We made meals out of anything edible we found. One day, we stumbled upon a plant that we used to eat leaves. After consuming them for dinner, however, we fell extremely ill. We thought we were going to die. We had misidentified the leaves and it turned out they were poisonous. We spent the night vomiting and feeling incredibly weak. The next day, we were too sick to go to work and had to take a day off. We were relieved that there were no Khmer Rouge present to monitor us. We were in charge of our actions, and we were grateful to be able to rest.

We spent about two months taking care of cotton plants. The job was not hard; however, the Khmer Rouge still barely provided us with enough food. A few weeks later when a second group of people just like us arrived to take our place, we relocated to a different job site.

1 9

The New Faction of Khmer Rouge –
Nearadae

U pon reaching the new location, I noticed a significant number of newcomers, including a different faction of the Khmer Rouge who referred to themselves as Nearadae. Somehow, they were different, they seemed to have lighter skin, were more mature, and spoke in a manner distinct from the previous group. It was puzzling to witness the existence of multiple factions within the Khmer Rouge, and it was unclear who was worse than the other. It seemed that the previous group had disappeared, and tension was palpable among the different factions. They did not get along with each other since there was more than one party of the Khmer Rouge.

A couple of hours later, I was told to go to the shelter managed by the Khmer Rouge. I could not help but feel anxious about my safety and the purpose of their summons. When I got to their shelter, I encountered two women in their late twenties who identified themselves as Nearadae. They were casually enjoying peanuts and soft drinks, and surprisingly, they were polite and friendly toward me. They instructed me to take a seat and one of them inquired about the number of individuals in my recently arrived group. I cautiously responded that there were ten of us. The other handed me a book that appeared to be a register for recording the names of people from various parts of the province. My mind raced with curiosity, yet I remained uncertain about their intentions. What should I say? All I knew was that the Khmer Rouge harbored deep animosity towards those who were educated, wealthy, and held government positions.

They told me not to be worried. They just wanted me to assist them in organizing a group of 100 people from all the recent arrivals and continued to reassure me not to be afraid. My thoughts were muddled. How did they know I could help, and why did they especially choose me? To make sense of the situation, I took one of their books. They provided me with instructions to form a group consisting of 10 people with a single leader, 30 people with a single leader, three groups of 30 people with a single leader, and three of 30 people, each with its leader.

Over the next few weeks, I found myself working and sharing meals with them daily and their food was great. People passing by their shelter noticed our activities and grew curious, wondering what role I played alongside those Nearedae.

One day while I was working for them, a male Nearadae's leader arrived. He had an arrogant demeanor, and fair skin, and appeared to be about 30 years old. I didn't like his attitude at all. He began questioning the female Nearadae about me and insisted that they leave the shelter. I overheard him asking why I was allowed to work with them and who I was. He left shortly thereafter. This encounter left me feeling anxious and unsettled.

During the time I worked with them, I noticed that they were humming songs from the past and these kinds of music were prohibited. As I got to know the two females Nearadae deeper, one of them told me that she was a college professor who got involved with communists a few years before the Khmer Rouge took control of Phnom Penh, Cambodia's capital. She paused because she had no idea how it would end and regretted being involved with the Khmer Rouge. She was the second individual to tell me of their circumstances. She must have trusted me enough to tell me her secrets. I was aware that she found it difficult to hold onto something that was significant, bothered her greatly, and made her hesitant to speak with anyone. I was able to get a little relief from listening to her. I changed the subject because I knew she didn't want to continue, and I didn't want her to feel awkward.

I inquired as to why she asked me to assist her rather than others. She told me that the Ungaleer assigned her here after she spent a few months in the village Phum Sroa Moch where my parents lived. She said that my dad was cute because Nearadaes liked to imitate and make fun of him because of his accent, but he didn't get mad at them; he just smiled. Additionally, she was aware of my family history.

After wrapping up aiding her, she appointed me to be in charge of a group of 99 people that I needed to supervise, with a few of them coming from the same village.

As group leaders, we were instructed to assign each person the task of removing dirt from one location to another to construct levees, which included digging dirt with a hoe and yoke. Each day, the surface had to be finished seven feet long by five feet wide and two and a half feet deep. Each leader of a group had to show up at the place of work at the dawn of the prior day to make sure that daily assignments were completed. For my part, I had to find a way to help my groups avoid trouble because I was aware that this task could be accomplished, but not by everyone.

Nearadae had designated a few individuals to prepare food and water for everyone. Each group leader was responsible for collecting food for their members at lunch or dinner. Each person would be provided with a bowl of cooked rice, salt, or whatever else they could provide that day. I delivered water to each person at the job site to make sure that everyone in my group had enough water.

I was competent and had this kind of work experience. I told my group that we had to complete our assignments each day; if we didn't, the next day, they would add more on top of what we could not finish. If that were the case, more and more would add up. I informed them that to avoid this issue, we needed to put in a lot of effort to determine the time of day, and we only wanted to finish by the end of the day, not earlier.

My group never had any issues over the days. We carried out our plans, and even when a few people fell behind, those who completed the task would assist one another. My group was the only one that always finished, which caused many other groups to discuss it. They wished to be a part of my group. I observed other groups beginning to have issues over the days. A growing number of people worked until late at night. During that time, I didn't do a lot of heavy work; rather, I organized more things to get them done on time every day.

We had already been there for about two months. One day, as I was going to get water for my group, I noticed that two male Nearadae were escorting the two female Nearadae I had worked with earlier when I first arrived, one of whom was the college professor. Because I knew who she was, I started to worry suddenly. They might have known what she thought of the Khmer Rouge. I worried about their safety. I was glad to meet her and learn that a few Khmer Rouge were forced to do things and couldn't refuse out of fear of endangering their lives.

About a week later, two new female Nearadae arrived. One was about my age and the other was in her late twenties.

Then late one evening, about 10 pm, one of my group members went to get water. She told me to flee as soon as she returned because, on her way to get water, she passed the Nearadae shelter. Out of curiosity, she listened as she heard my name mentioned. They were discussing my upbringing. She claimed that both male and female voices were heard. I knew right away that it had to be the male Nearadae's leader who was questioning me as I helped organize the group. When I saw the two females Nearadae being escorted a couple of weeks earlier, I remembered. My mind immediately advised me to flee. I was concerned that I might get lost, so I hurriedly requested the assistance of one of the girls in my group by the name of Rea, who came from the same village. She hesitated, but she eventually agreed because she also desired to return home.

Rea and I quickly gathered our belongings, so we didn't waste any time. Before I left, I thanked the girl who told me. I walked as quickly as I could because I was terrified for my life. I couldn't see much because it was dark. Currently, everyone was sleeping. The Khmer Rouge used bicycles to periodically patrol. We encountered a patrol bicycle after walking for about an hour. I recognized that it was the Khmer Rouge when I saw a light in the distance. I told Rea that we should conceal quickly, yet where?

When I turned around, I saw bushes nearby. I pointed "there" to the bushes. We quickly hid in the bushes.

My heart raced as the bicycle's light approached, and then the rider passed. We hugged each other in relief and continued to flee. We ran and walked until the sun came up. We did not want anyone to be suspicious of us now, so we decided to walk normally in the morning. We traveled through village after village without being noticed. Because we were wearing a black uniform and a nice scarf, which was only worn by the Khmer Rouge, people greeted us along the way. The leaders of the villagers graciously served us when we requested food because they thought we were members of the Khmer Rouge.

After expressing our gratitude for the meal, we made our way towards the village, which became visible from a distance after a long walk. I felt a sense of relief as I knew I was almost home. Since the flood season had ended, and the ground was too uneven, we didn't require a boat to return home. As evening approached, we reached the outskirts of the village, surrounded by vast corn fields that were not far from where my parents lived.

I wanted to wait until darkness shrouded the area, providing cover for my arrival. I found a hiding spot amidst the cornfield. From there, I could see a glimpse of my parent's house from a distance. Rea's parent's home was also near a cornfield, so she snuck her way back home first. Meanwhile, I remained hidden and stayed quiet. Just after a short while of waiting, I heard my father's voice calling for me to come out and assuring me that it was safe. He said we had a new group of Khmer Rouge, and they were much nicer. I questioned him about how he knew I was hiding. He explained that Rea's mother had told him of my presence in the cornfield. My father called out as we approached the front door to inform my mom that I had returned home. The atmosphere was filled with happiness, and my mom was overjoyed. I told my parents the purpose of my journey. They listened with deep concern when they heard my story.

The following morning, Mom went to work as usual. She rowed a boat around the river to search for water spinach, which grew on the edge of the river, a valuable vegetable for the villagers. The village's leader did not care what, where, or how my mother spent her time, as long as she brought back food

Mom often took the opportunity to cross over to the opposite side of the river when she finished finding food early in the day. As she explored the area, she met a woman who lived on the opposite side of the river. The woman knew my parents well, she came from a small town next to Mongkol Borey. They shared stories, and experiences, and became good friends.

The opposite side of the river was controlled by a different group of the Khmer Rouge. It was strictly forbidden, however, to cross over to the other side, as each province had its authority. The consequence of being caught and taken into custody would be severe.

When my mom got enough water spinach for the village, she took the time to meet the woman and requested for me to temporarily stay under her care, ensuring my safety. I didn't know all the details of their arrangement; all I knew was my mother had made this decision to protect me.

After arranging for me to move in with the woman, my parents didn't want to delay; they were afraid the new group of Khmer Rouge might come to Phum Sroa Moch to search for me. Once again, I said goodbye to my family. Before departing, I left behind my black uniform, shoes, and scarf, recognizing their value, and believing they could be handy in an emergency.

My mother and I went to the boat and rowed it across the river. Once we reached our destination, she concealed the boat amidst the shrubbery to prevent it from being taken.

To her friend's house, we walked for about an hour. I saw a house that was like ours in Mongkol Borey, but much smaller. At the point when we showed up, a woman of my mother's age emerged to welcome us. She shared a home with her husband, son, and daughter-in-law. Mom told me that she would come to get me once she was sure it was safe and introduced me to the family of her friend. After a proper introduction and thanks, Mom needed to return. She told me to not worry about anything at all, just to take care of myself.

I was treated well by the woman and her family. They gave me food and shelter while they kept me hidden in her house. A few weeks later, two of the spies for the Khmer Rouge who were in the area carried out their typical home inspections. I had no time to hide because it came as a surprise. The woman told them that I was her relative but had lost all my family, so she took me in. I was informed that an Ungaleer would not permit a young person to remain at home and that I belonged to a labor camp. Because it was rice harvest season and the village required as much assistance as possible, the woman requested that I remain in the community until finishing harvesting rice. They agreed but demanded that I immediately pack and relocate to where the young people stayed. The woman told me not to be concerned. After packing up, she walked me to the place of work and told a few of the women who were there to assist her in taking care of me because I was new to the area and did not yet know anyone. The woman was known for her kindness and compassion. I shared a shelter with several other women. I was surprised to see that the Khmer Rouge in this part of this province was the same as previous, no Nearadae.

The following morning, I was given a sickle, which each person held in their hands. When we arrived at the location, the rice crops that needed to be harvested stretched for miles and miles, all of which were in the water. Several boats were ready to take us there. Each boat could only carry 4-5 of us before the risk of sinking. It took about 5 minutes to get to the field. If we chose to walk, it took about 20 minutes or so. It was so cool in the early morning to get into the water as deep as our hips. We harvested the rice and loaded it onto the boat.

At the point when it was full, the individual accountable for moving the rice would row the boat and drop it off on land.

Our lunch was initially delivered by boat. When we were eating while standing in the water, it was not at all convenient, so we requested to eat ashore. The next day we returned by boat to the land for lunch, and they served us each a cup of cooked rice. We were responsible for locating our protein and vegetables. As a result, every day when we were working in the water, we would pick up anything that could be eaten. We occasionally stepped on fish, small crabs, snails, and so forth. Every day when we worked, it was very cold, but we could only try to finish the work as quickly as possible.

Then, on one occasion early in the day while working, I stepped on something delicate, and it moved. I thought I got a good-sized fish, and I was overjoyed. I responded rapidly to no one's surprise and put my head down in the water as my hand reached and crab that was under my feet. I got frightened and threw it as far as I could when it emerged from the water. It seemed to be a snake. I was shaking. I rushed toward the boat and requested that the Khmer Rouge permit me to get on the boat for a few minutes. I explained what had occurred to me. After she learned as to why, she allowed me to get on her boat. I sat for a while on the boat to calm down and thought, "Was that a snake?" It could have been an eel, but I would never know for sure. I still did not like it, even if it was an eel. Working inside the water all day long was very difficult.

Every day, I felt like I was about to turn to ice. I experienced that when I stayed in the water all day, my body would feel warmer, but it got very cold as I got out. We had harvested so much rice after just a few weeks. As days went by, we heard gunfire every day, and it appeared that the Khmer Rouge were less and less interested in watching us work.

2 0

Freedom at Last

It was about 50 degrees in the rice field. It was a typical climate at this time of the year. It was breezy and cold in the morning. For days, we could hear gun battles louder than usual. Of course, we had no idea who was fighting with whom or about what, but we always believed that it was a good thing to hear about. It gave us some hope to look forward to the future. We believed that somewhere, and somehow, some people out there were fighting to rescue us from this nightmare.

One day, we arrived at work around 5 am as normal. There was no Khmer Rouge there to watch over us, so we just did our job as usual. Even when it reached noon, there was no sign of any Khmer Rouge at all. It was just too weird. After a while, we decided that one of us would have to find out why they were not there to watch over us all day.

An hour later, he returned and informed us that he saw the Khmer Rouge packing their belongings and that they would return to the woods. There were mixed emotions for all of us. We wondered what was going on. Deep down inside our minds, we believed that it was a good thing. But we were afraid to act just yet.

And then, not too far away from our work sight, we saw hundreds of Khmer Rouge walking in line quietly toward the woods just like we heard. They carried whatever they could with them. We were overwhelmed with joy to see that. We took a break from doing anything and stood there in the water silently watching them leave. It was a long line and a few hours later, they finally disappeared in the woods. We looked at each other then started to yell and scream with so much joy and ran back to the land as fast as we could.

Finally, we had our freedom back after these years. Unfortunately, a tragic thing happened to a few of us. Some of us were so excited that we forgot to take any precautions and did not realize that there might be some of the Khmer Rouge members still around. One of the men, about fifty years old, had managed to hide a radio from the Khmer Rouge for all these years and he could not wait any longer to finally turn it on and hear an update from Phnom Penh.

He got his radio out and turned it on to listen to the news quietly. A few of the Khmer Rouge were on their way walking toward the woods. They walked by the man's shed and listened in. They were so angry that they pulled out their guns and shot and killed the man. The two people were in love for some time, but they were not able to talk to each other due to the rules and regulations of the Ugarleer. Finally, they were able to find each other and were caught by the Khmer Rouge as well. Both were shot and killed. Even though there were only a few left, they all had guns. Therefore, we were still afraid of them. The unexpected killings alarmed all of us to take all necessary precautions until we knew that we were safe.

No one had to go to work anymore, at least for the time being. After all, this was the first time we had time off in the past 4 plus years. We were all able to eat rice the way we wanted and when we wanted it. We were able to talk about anything we wanted without fearing for our lives. Youth and adults alike had been waiting for this day for so long and finally, it was here. Everyone had plans for their future.

As for me, my plan was to be united with my family. But I had no idea where they were. How was I going to find them? Would I find them? What would happen to me if I could not find them? All these questions rose in my thoughts once again. I decided to talk to the people that I stayed with. I told them that I wanted to search for my family. They told me not to worry, my family would find me. They knew where I was, and I didn't know where they were. If I was going to look for them, where would I go? All of this made sense to me, so I listened to them. I hoped that my family would find me. The whole village was celebrating every day. It was just like an old-time before the Khmer Rouge took control of the country.

Another two days had gone by, and I had been waiting impatiently. The next morning, I was sitting among a group of people in front of the house. We were baking sweet potatoes at the campfire cheering and sharing the happiness of freedom and I tried to cheer up along with them, but it was difficult for me. I constantly wished that my family would just appear in front of me so that we all could be together again as a family.

Later that morning, I heard my younger brother's voice calling me. Was I dreaming? I turned around to look for the voice. Then I was overwhelmed to find that my wish had been grand. I saw my twelve-year-old brother with his bicycle less than five hundred feet away from me. There was tons of blissfulness inside me. I was so happy to see him, and I ran toward him. I asked him, how did he know I was there? My brother told me that the whole family knew where I was, and our parents sent him to get me. He told me that he knew the road well. It was just like I was told by my hosts; my family would find me. I rushed inside the house and told them that my brother was here and that I needed to go with him now. My hosts understood that I had been waiting long enough to be united with my family. They agreed to let me go. I thank them for their hospitality.

I rode the bicycle while my brother sat in the back. We rode on the roadway across several towns, and we saw many of the Vietnamese troops patrolling the roads. They all carried guns, some sat on army trucks while others walked around in the town.

I was a bit scared, but my brother told me not to be afraid. These troops were not the same as the Khmer Rouge; they would not harm us. He told me that when he was on his way to find me, these troops had given him some food. They seemed friendly but they did not speak Cambodian.

After several hours of biking, we approached the border of Phnom Buntew Neag. It was the moment that I had been waiting for. Shortly after, we got off our bicycle and walked toward one of the small sheds that were made from hay and wood. My brother pointed to the shed and said, "That's our home." The shed was as big as a bedroom. That was one of the best homes that we lived in so far since we were evacuated from our home in Monkolborey.

2 1

Family Reunion

I was in such high spirits when I finally arrived and saw my family together. I was home at last. I looked around our shed. There was not much room in there, but we were filled with joy.

After sharing all the bad and good news, I learned that while my mom was at Phum Sroa Moch, she was able to use her knowledge of acupressure to release people's headaches and other minor aches and pains. The result was so amazing that people in the village started to talk about them. It seemed simple, but other villagers tried to copy her technique and the outcome was different. People showed their appreciation by giving her some rice each time they needed her help.

Mom also confided in me that she had a recurring dream where she witnessed the entire process of childbirth, including the necessary steps involved. However, the abundance of blood in the dream made her uncomfortable, and she was hesitant to accept the knowledge presented to her in her dream. In my thoughts, since there was no physician present, it could be God's way of calling her to serve as a midwife.

According to her, the passing months only worsened the situation as rations were reduced from one cup to half a cup of uncooked rice per person. Mom was able to use the black uniform and scarf that I left for them to exchange with villagers for some rice, but it was only temporary relief. This begged the question, what happened to the rice that was harvested every year? The answer lay in the hands of the communist Khmer Rouge, who implemented this tactic of control through starvation. Despite this, some regions of the country fared better than others, with the prosperity of each province largely dependent on its leader. My parents were fortunate enough to learn that one of their former employees resided in the relatively prosperous region of Phnom Buntew Neag where there was still food. Crossing over to the other section of the province, however, was strictly prohibited.

To survive, my family devised a plan to escape from Phum Sroa Moch when the situation was at its worst. With no food left for the people, they were forced to share one can of rice among the entire family. To stretch the limited rations, Mom had to search for edible weeds to cook with the rice, adding extra amounts of water to increase the volume of the food. Even something as simple as water spinach was all gone. There were too many people demanding food. On rare occasions, she was able to obtain banana trunks to use as food. Although not intended for human consumption, the trunks of banana plants were chopped into small pieces and fed to pigs. Under the cover of darkness, my parents plotted their escape.

To escape, my family had to cross to the other side of the river. Luckily, Mom's assignments to find water spinach for the Khmer Rouge had provided her with access to a boat, which she had hidden behind bushes in the river. It was the day of escaping from Phum Sroa Moch; my family waited until midnight when everyone was asleep to sneak out quietly. Upon arriving at the riverbank, however, they realized that the boat was missing. Fear gripped them as they knew that crossing the river without a boat would be impossible. While every member of the family could swim, my mother was not a proficient swimmer, adding to their anxiety.

In their haste to escape, my family had brought along a few of my household items, including pots and pans.

However, my father's panic set in as he worried that the Khmer Rouge might discover their plan and execute them all. Sensing the urgency of the situation, my older brother volunteered to search for a boat while the rest of the family hid quietly next to a bush. After half an hour had elapsed with no sign of his return, fear and anxiety mounted among my family members. They wondered if he had found a boat or if he had been caught by the Khmer Rouge. The waiting was agonizing, and another half an hour ticked by without any sign of my brother's return. My father suggested that they abandon the plan and try again another day, but Mom disagreed. She reminded him that arrangements had already been made for their escape that day and that a man named Harn was waiting for them in a small town on the other side of the river. She urged him to do whatever it took to reach the destination, even if it meant taking risks.

My parents had previously made arrangements with Mr. Harn, a former employee of my dad's, who was a truck driver living in Phnom Buntew Neag. He knew how to navigate the Khmer Rouge regime, having lived in Phnom Buntew Neag before they took over. He had convinced the Khmer Rouge to allow my family to move to Phnom Buntew Neag, given the sensitive politics involved in crossing towns or villages. The Khmer Rouge had agreed to allow my family to stay in Phnom

Buntew Neag if they could escape from Phum Sroa Moch with one condition.

The Khmer Rouge leader had demanded a watch as a condition for my family's safe passage to Phnom Buntew Neag. Although my parents did not have a watch, they were confident that they would be able to find one. They knew that my brother-in-law had previously worked as a watch repairman before the Khmer Rouge took control of the country. Therefore, my parents believed that if they managed to get permission from the Khmer Rouge leader in Phnom Buntew Neag, they could find my sister in Phum Makast and she would help them locate a watch to satisfy the condition set forth by the Khmer Rouge leader.

The wait for my brother's return took nearly two hours, and during that time, my parents anxiously kept looking at the river. With the help of the moon's light, they could see far and hoped to catch a glimpse of my brother's return. My dad, however, began to lose patience and grew increasingly worried that the Khmer Rouge might spot them trying to sneak out, which could result in all deaths. Meanwhile, Mom silently prayed that the Khmer Rouge would not discover them hiding and that my brother would return safely. The tension in the air was palpable, and every passing moment felt like an eternity as they waited for a sign of hope.

After another half hour of waiting, my parents' fear for my brother's safety continued to grow. With no sign of his return, they looked at each other for an answer, but neither had anything to say. The sense of hope began to diminish, and the atmosphere became tense. Mom looked up at the moonlight and silently prayed for her son's safe return. Suddenly, the shadow of my brother's boat could be seen in the distance, and Mom's prayer was seemingly answered. It was a prominent relieved to the whole family, and without wasting any time, they all quietly and quickly got on the boat. Although the river crossing didn't take long, the boat was not big enough for one trip, so they had to make two trips to avoid sinking. My mom, two of my youngest brothers, and some of their belongings got on the first trip. As they unloaded their belongings from the boat, my mother instructed my brothers to remain quiet and hide in the bushes in case someone saw them. Mom's heart pounded with fear of being caught by the Khmer Rouge in the middle of their escape. Her attention was on the rest of the family waiting on the other side of the river, and she knew that they had to move quickly to ensure everyone's safety.

In the meantime, my 5-year-old youngest brother found a place to hide in the field. Finally, everyone arrived at the same side of the river as my mom. Quietly and quickly, they got out of the boat, gathered their belongings, and continued their journey on foot. They walked through the rice fields which were about 4 feet high. After about fifteen minutes of walking, Mom realized that my youngest brother was missing. They panicked and began frantically searching for him, but he was nowhere to be found. Fear for his safety consumed them, and they quietly whispered his name, hoping to hear a response.

After what felt like an eternity, they finally heard his faint reply. He was hiding in the bushes, which were much taller than him and had been too scared to come out. My parents were filled with both relief and admiration for their brave son. They hugged him tightly, and together, they continued their journey with a newfound sense of gratitude for their safety and each other's company.

After several hours of walking, they finally arrived at their destination, where a small home was waiting for them. As per their prior arrangement, Mr. Harn had obtained a permission slip from the Khmer Rouge and a bicycle, allowing my dad to travel to Phum Makast to obtain a watch from my sister.

Despite the dangers that still loomed around them, my dad set off on his journey to retrieve the watch. It was a risky move, but it was worth it. After what felt like an eternity, my dad finally returned with the watch, and the family was overjoyed to have this small piece of hope and normalcy in their lives.

Although their journey was far from over, this moment represented a small victory for them amid the chaos and uncertainty of their situation. It gave them the strength and determination to keep going, to keep fighting for their survival and their freedom.

I was just so happy that I was able to join my family again at last. Our new lives started the next morning. I woke up at about 6 am. Breakfast was already waiting for us. Our lunches were also packed and ready to go. My siblings and I grabbed our rice-cutting knives and headed to the rice field, ready to work. This time, things were different. There was no one to tell us what to do or when to do it. We were free to work at our own pace and keep as much of the rice crop as we could harvest.

Working in the fields was hard, but it was a sense of freedom that we had not experienced in a long time. We worked diligently, side by side, with a newfound sense of purpose and determination. As we harvested the rice crop, we felt a sense of accomplishment and pride in our hard work.

Despite the challenges that still lay ahead, we were grateful for this new beginning, for the chance to rebuild our lives and our family. We knew that it would not be easy, but we were ready to face whatever challenges came our way, knowing that we had each other and the strength to keep going.

Every day in the rice fields, the looming threat of a landmine explosion weighed heavily on our minds. With no knowledge of where the explosive devices were buried, we were acutely aware of the potential danger that awaited us each time we stepped foot on the land. Despite our fears, we persevered and worked tirelessly to harvest enough rice to sustain our family for months. While mom urged caution and concern for us to stop our work, my older brother and I were determined to gather as much rice as possible. Meanwhile, my father met with other concerned adults to discuss the perilous situation in our country.

After weeks of collecting rice, we finally had enough food to last us six months. My father, however, called a family meeting and announced that we must leave the country due to ongoing danger and uncertainty. My brother protested, arguing that we couldn't just abandon our harvest. But carrying such a large quantity of rice with us would be impractical, so my parents suggested we donate it to Mr. Harn. After much discussion, we ultimately agreed and left with heavy hearts, uncertain of what the future held.

After donating most of our rice harvest to Mr. Harn and his family, we departed from Phnom Buntew Neag the following morning. There were many people on the road traveling in different directions searching for a better and safer place to live just like us. The journey to our hometown of Montgol Borei took several hours, and upon arrival, we discovered that our home had been occupied by multiple families. With no proof of ownership, the property was claimed on a first-come, first-served basis. Unable to stay, we traveled to the nearby town of Svay where my oldest sister resided before the Khmer Rouge took control. The only available space for us, however, was the front porch of someone else's property, where we huddled together for warmth and shelter.

Several days later, my parents expressed a desire to reunite with my older sister, Eng, her husband, and their two children. My father and I took on a day-long journey by foot to locate their whereabouts and convince them to join us. Eventually, we succeeded in convincing them, along with Eng's in-laws' family, to join us under the porch of our temporary home. Despite the cramped living conditions, we were grateful to be together as a family once again.

2 2

Selling Cupcakes

L ife had become reminiscent of the past, as everyone struggled to make ends meet. The outdoor market was open to the public, and with no currency in circulation, goods were exchanged for rice or other highly demanded items such as bicycles, which could be traded for gold. For example, a single piece of clothing could be sold for three cans of rice or a bicycle, which could then be exchanged for 0.02 ozs of gold.

As weeks passed, our food supplies got low, and we faced the harsh reality that we would soon run out of food to eat. It became clear that we needed to take action or risk starvation.

One night, around 3 am, the Khmer Rouge infiltrated our town, and their intentions were unclear. The sudden appearance of the Khmer Rouge caused widespread fear among the residents, and it was not long before a gun battle broke out between them and Vietnamese troops. The fight lasted for about an hour, resulting in several casualties among the citizens.

The following morning, my parents and many other families decided to leave the town and move to another location called Ourmbele. This new location was one step closer to the border of Thailand, and many people were looking for shelter. It was a first-come, first-served situation. However, my family found our shelter under a large tree.

Despite the difficult circumstances, my father and other adults continued to gather daily to discuss how to safely leave the country. He believed that there were still many dangers in Cambodia and that it was imperative for us to leave. The closest country that was accessible for us to travel to was Thailand, which we could reach by foot. With this in mind, we prepared ourselves for the grueling journey ahead, filled with uncertainty and danger.

With our food supplies running low, my brother and his friends decided to go fishing for food. Meanwhile, my mother, sister, and I put our baking skills to use and started making cupcakes (num akar) to sell at the outdoor market. Since there was no sugar available, we had to get creative and found a tree near our shelter that produced fruit we could use as a sugar substitute. When the fruit was ripped, it would drop from the tree. We collected, cleaned, and soaked them in water for a few hours. We would extract the juice and use it as a sweetened base for our cakes. While the cakes were not as sweet as those made with sugar, they were still delicious for people to enjoy.

Every morning, my mother and sister would wake up at about 2 am to begin making the cupcakes, and by 6 am, I would take them to the outdoor market to sell. Each cupcake sold for one can of rice, and it did not take long for me to sell all fifty cakes that my mother and sister had made. By 11 am, all of our cakes had been sold, and I felt a sense of pride and accomplishment knowing that I had contributed to helping our family. I initially felt embarrassed selling cupcakes; every time I saw someone that I knew, or who knew me, I would hide my face from them so that they would not notice that I was selling cupcakes. I soon realized that it was a necessary means of survival and that there was no shame in working hard to make ends meet.

After my cupcake business grew in popularity, others began to imitate the idea, and before long, competitions were being held in the market. The cupcake stock that once took me only a few hours to sell, now took me all day. My sister, however, had a new suggestion.

She proposed that we take our cakes to sell in the nearby village of Phum Makak where she had lived during the Khmer Rouge's control of the country. Since the village was not too far from us, she believed that there would not be much competition and that we could tap into a new customer base. Furthermore, not everyone had access to the market, and there were many children in the village who would enjoy our cakes.

The following morning, we woke up bright and early at 5 am, eager to continue our cupcake business in Phum Makak. We carefully packed our cakes into a large basket, and I rode my bicycle while my sister sat in the back and held the basket steady.

After an hour and a half of cycling, we arrived at the village, where we were greeted with warm welcomes and smiles. The villagers were happy to see my sister, and even happier to see that we had brought food to them instead of them having to go to the market to get it. The children in the village were especially excited to see our cupcakes, and quickly gathered around us.

To our surprise, it did not take long at all for us to sell out of our cupcakes. In just about an hour, all our cakes were gone, and we had a big bag of rice to take back home. The success we had in Phum Makak was much faster than we had expected, and we knew that we had tapped into a new market. From that day forward, we continued to sell our cupcakes in Phum Makak, and the village became a loyal customer base. Our cupcake business had not only helped us survive but had also become a means of bringing joy and happiness to others.

A few weeks after our successful cupcake business in Phum Makak, my father broke the news to us that we had to move closer to the border in preparation for our escape to Thailand. This meant that we had to leave behind our shelter and all our belongings, including the food we had worked hard to gather

Although it was difficult to leave behind our hard-earned food, we knew that survival was our top priority. We gathered what we could carry and made the journey to the border, leaving behind our shelter, our belongings, and our cupcakes business.

2 3

The Escaping Night Terror

As the day of our escape approached, my family and many others who were also preparing to leave gathered around. The next morning, we set out as early as 5 am, joining hundreds of people on the road who were all seeking a new home and a better life. Again, there were miles of people on the road marching out from Cambodia trying to find a new home.

With limited resources, every family had to use whatever means of transportation they could find. Bicycles and cow wagons were the most popular vehicles, and the only two types of transportation available. Families with bicycles would load whatever they could carry onto their bikes. Fortunately, my family was lucky enough to have a cow with a wagon, which allowed us to load most of our food and belongings onto the wagon, and mom and little brother ride alongside.

Those who did not have a bike or cow wagon would carry their belongings on their heads or shoulders, bravely facing the challenges of the journey ahead. We walked all day long trying to get to our destination before sunset. We took a rest several times so that our cow could take a break as well. It was nearly dawn when we arrived at the town called Phum Nement. I was surprised to see many families had gotten there before us. Some of them arrived there shortly after Vietnam's troops took control of the country. The objective we all shared was to search for a secure place in which we could stay until an opportunity presented itself to escape. Thailand was the sole neighboring country within reach by foot.

My family was able to find a place to shelter until the next plan. It was under the big mango tree in front of one of the country homes. Not far away from the tree, there was a small pond full of water lilies near the roadway. While other members of my family were unloading stuff, Mom and I were preparing for dinner. We looked for a big rock to use as a cooking stove and some dead tree branches nearby as a campfire. It did not take us long to have dinner ready.

Everyone was exhausted and off to sleep after dinner. All of us together included my older sister, her in-law, her husband, and their two young sons. The older one was four years old and the younger was 8 months old. Together, we were 22 people that rested under the mango tree. A few feet away from us, there were some other families. It was at least a couple of miles along the roadside that were filled with people.

A couple of hours later, everyone was sleeping, and I was still awake. I looked around and I saw some burning wood light leftover from cooking. Some cows were still standing while others sat and rested. I looked at our wagon. The bed of the wagon seemed very comfortable to sleep on. I decided to get up from the ground walk to the wagon and sleep on it. After a while, I fell asleep.

It was about 3 am when I suddenly was awakened by the sound of the gun battle. The bullets were flying in front of me just like raindrops. I was so frightened. I jumped down so fast from the bed of the wagon and crawled to stay in the group with my family. The bullets were dropping constantly around us. I prayed for the bullets to stay away from us. Next to me were my sister and her two children. They were so frightened by the sound of the bullets. We were so lucky that my two nephews did not cry at all. I could imagine what would happen if one of them cried. After about fifteen minutes of gun battle,

I heard footsteps not far away from me. The sounds got closer and closer. I was afraid to look at who that was. Then, the footsteps stop near me. I opened my eyes and saw several feet with black rubber shoes. I knew right away; they were the Khmer Rouge. Were we going to die? The question arose in my mind, and I feared for our lives.

Then I heard one of them say "There are many people here, should we kill them all?" This is it! There was no way to escape with our lives now. The Khmer Rouge hated us because we were happy when the Vietnamese troops took control over Phnom Penh, the capital of Cambodia, and we had our freedom back and they had to flee to the woods. "Kill them all, kill them," one of them replied. "Burn them, pour the gasoline, and burn them alive" was another Khmer Rouge suggestion. Then there was the sound of the army tanks and trucks approaching. "We won't have time, they are coming. Hurry... go back in the woods," one of them shouted out. They then returned to where they came from.

Gun battles between the Khmer Rouge and Vietnamese troops were still going on for another hour before they finally ended. The terrifying sounds were everywhere. I could hear people crying because members of their families were killed or hurt by the bullets. Some of the cows were killed or hit by the gunfire as well. It was light enough outside from the moon that I could see the people who were resting on the right side of my family were shot. I looked at the left side, several people got hurt. It did not matter which direction I turned; I saw someone hurt. God had been blessing my family that stayed under the mango tree, we were all safe. Then my brother-in-law and my younger brother came out from the lily pond, they were all wet. They were hiding in the pond. Assuming the Khmer Rouge were to kill us around then, the main two individuals that were still alive were them.

I felt heartbroken witnessing the harm and death caused by the terrible events. I wished nobody had to suffer such tragedies. Then, I heard crying coming from across the street where many people had gathered. It turned out that a family who had slept under a mosquito net was killed by the Khmer Rouge. The parents were brutally killed by having their stomachs opened. The Khmer Rouge despised them for sleeping under the mosquito net, believing that only the wealthy did so. The wailing and sobbing of those who lost their loved ones was like thunder, and the wounded cows mooed in pain from the gunfire. It was a truly sorrowful scene.

For those who were safe, families embraced each other. We are all depressed from the terrifying night. We never expected that the plan for a better life would turn out to be a nightmare. The Vietnamese troops then announced that we must return to where we came from. No one would be allowed to stay because they believed that the Khmer Rouge would return. No one wanted to take any chances, so rushedly we packed our belongings and returned to Ourmbele.

Upon our arrival, we found out that another family had already taken shelter under our resting tree. We had no choice but to look for a new place to stay, and eventually settled for a location that wasn't as ideal as our previous one. My sister and I continued to sell cupcakes to make ends meet, while my brother and his friends went fishing to gather some food.

2 4

The Escape

A few months later, my family and many others took on a journey to Phum Nemet again. When we got there before dawn, we saw that hundreds of other families had already arrived. We searched for a shelter, and we found the same big mango tree that we stayed under last time. Mom said this tree protected us last time, so we would stay there again. We settled in and waited for the right time to make our move. Every day, my dad met with other adults for planning while my brother and a few others went to look for a place to fish.

A month later, Dad told us that in two more nights, we would have to escape to Thailand. My brothers, sisters and I were concerned because we were afraid that the escape plan would fail and that we would be in great danger once again. Dad said that the escape would be risky but possible, and there would be people who knew the way well. We had to pay them with gold to be able to go, but we didn't have gold left because the Khmer Rouge had taken most of it. Fortunately, my older sister had hidden her gold from the Khmer Rouge and was able to use it to pay for her family and us. We packed only the necessary things for the journey, prepared food, and water for the night, and left the rest of our belongings behind.

We were so nervous and excited about this plan that we could not sleep at all. We were waiting for the right time to start our escape. Midnight arrived; 10 families were meeting up with the person who was in charge of the escape. We followed the man and walked quietly into the woods, continually until the sun rose and we were very tired. We rested when we could, but we had to use our food and water sparingly or we would risk running out before we reached Thailand, and we would be starvation.

Unfortunately, a few of the older people began to faint from exhaustion, and some of us started to feel unstable from lack of food and water. The worst part was when the person leading us suddenly disappeared.

Now everybody, young and adults, panicked, and we realized that we had been scammed. Some of the adults tried to calm down and figure out a solution. After they analyzed it, they decided we should continue our own and hope to find our way.

As the day turned into night, we were all very scared and anxious. We had no idea where we were, and we were lost in the woods with no food or water. It was getting late; which made us even more afraid to not know where we were going. Everyone was feeling hopeless and depressed, and some adults were becoming delirious from lack of food and water. We knew that we had to do something, or we would not survive. We continued to walk for what felt like hours, but we could not find any hope. The darkness was closing in on us, and we were all getting very tired. Suddenly, we heard a noise in the distance, and we were all scared. Then we heard footsteps. Were those wild animals? For a moment we were frightened that possibly tigers or something else might have us for their meal. We paused, the steps got closer, and then we saw a forty-some-year-old man with a weapon. But he did not look like the Khmer Rouge, that was a huge relief. An adult called him to ask if he knew how to reach a roadway or any close by town. The man did not speak Cambodian, he was Thai. Thank goodness one of the adults on our journey could speak Thai! He and the Thai man were communicating, and we learned that he was a hunter, searching for his food. After many questions back and forth, the Thai hunter would show us the right way to reach the roadway, but he wanted to be paid. We did not have any more choice except to make things happen. The adults gathered, figuring out how to pay him with the only thing they had, which was gold. I did not know how much they paid, or who paid but he accepted the offer. He agreed to lead the way.

The Thai hunter led the way. We followed him for about three hours, and we started to hear the sound of cars, we were so thrilled. Excitement filled our hearts as we realized our new home was within reach. At this moment, we glance at each other with joy. Not long after, we could see the road from a distance, with cars and trucks driving by. The man wished us luck and he proceeded to his hunting. After all our efforts, this escape had become victorious. We hurriedly made our way towards the road, but our success was short-lived as we were suddenly surrounded and arrested by the Thai border patrol.

About the Author

KC was born in a small town in Mongkol Borey, province of Banteay Meanchey, Cambodia. She was 15 years old when her life took a drastic turn when the Khmer Rouge seized control of the country overnight. As a result, the entire population was evacuated to the countryside, and everyone was forced to become farmers. The Khmer Rouge, following their communist ideology, began targeting and eliminating individuals they deemed "worthless" due to their education.

During her early teenage years, from 1975 to 1979, KC endured a tumultuous life under the oppressive regime of the Khmer Rouge. Those five years were filled with uncertainty, as she lived each day without knowing what might happen to her- whether she would survive or perish. KC spent most of her time toiling in labor camps. She consumed whatever meager sustenance she could find just to survive.

The Khmer Rouge regime eventually fell when they were defeated by Vietnamese troops, marking the return of freedom for the people. Even in light of this, hardships continued to plague KC's family. In a desperate bid for a better life, her father decided to escape to Thailand, a mere 50 kilometers (31 miles) away. What should have been a short drive in modern times turned into a treacherous, months-long ordeal for those pursuing the same goal. They faced imminent danger, with bombs exploding nearby while they took cover in trenches. Many lost their lives, but KC's family managed to escape the horrors that surrounded them.

Eventually, KC and her family found solace and settled down in the United States.

New challenges now awaited her. Learning a new language proved to be a major hurdle as she had to adapt to a different culture. Despite speaking limited English, KC found herself taking a low-paying job, working in a flower shop as a cleaner, and picking blueberries on weekends, all while striving to improve her language skills.

After getting married, KC and her husband ventured into crafting handcrafted silver jewelry. They both worked multiple jobs just to make ends meet. She also took a part-time role as a teacher's aide through the international classroom program.

Her passion for sharing her experiences led her to accept a speaking engagement arranged by a friend at an International Classroom setting. Some teenagers in her audience were moved to tears upon hearing her speeches, realizing how fortunate they were compared to KC. Some of the audience encouraged and suggested she write a book and share her story with the world. Due to her limited English writing skills and the absence of formal training, however, she put the idea on hold for many years.

Finally, with the encouragement of friends and family, KC decided to write the story you are about to read. English writing remained a challenge for her, and she often struggled to comprehend the meaning of words she searched online. With the help of her children, however, she painstakingly pieced together her narrative and transformed it into a book. Simple tasks that would take 15 minutes for others required her one to two weeks of effort.

The night became sleepless as she worked on her story, driven by eagerness to share it with the world and impart the message that no matter how arduous life may be, we must always preserve and move forward.

www.myselffree.com

Acknowledgments

I would like to express my deepest gratitude to Mrs. Conroy, Sue Dyke, and Prema for providing me with the opportunity to share my life experience under the Khmer Rouge regime through an International Classroom program. It was through this program that I found the platform to tell my story and raise awareness about the atrocities committed during that time. I am truly thankful for their support and guidance throughout this journey.

I would also like to extend my heartfelt appreciation to my husband, whose unwavering encouragement has been a constant source of strength for me. His belief in me and my story has been instrumental in shaping this book.

I am grateful to my children for their invaluable assistance in editing and refining my narrative. Their patience, dedication, and insightful suggestions have significantly enhanced the quality of this book. I am proud to have them by my side, supporting me every step of the way.

Lastly, I want to express my deep appreciation to my sister, Jane. Her unwavering support and encouragement have been a constant source of motivation for me, and I am grateful for her presence in my life.

To all those who have played a part in bringing this book to life, I am forever grateful. Your contributions have made a significant impact, and I am truly honored to have had your support throughout this journey.

Thanks for reading!

Please add a short review on Amazon and let me know what you think!